# Michael T. Battis

## COGNITION-BASED ASSESSMENT & TEACHING

### of Place Value

# Building on
# Students'
# Reasoning

## HEINEMANN
Portsmouth, NH

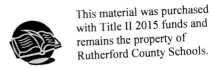

**Heinemann**

361 Hanover Street

Portsmouth, NH 03801–3912

www.heinemann.com

*Offices and agents throughout the world*

**Library of Congress Cataloging-in-Publication Data**

Battista, Michael T.

   Cognition-based assessment and teaching of place value : building on students' reasoning / Michael Battista.

      p. cm.

   Includes bibliographical references.

   ISBN-13: 978-0-325-04343-2

   ISBN-10: 0-325-04343-4

   1. Place value (Mathematics)—Study and teaching (Elementary). 2. Arithmetic—Study and teaching (Elementary). 3. Reasoning—Study and teaching (Elementary). 4. Thought and thinking—Study and teaching (Elementary). 5. Cognitive learning. I. Title.

QA141.15.B34 2012

372.7'2—dc23
                                                                2011043545

*Editor:* Katherine Bryant

*Production:* Victoria Merecki

*Typesetter:* Publishers' Design & Production Services, Inc.

*Interior and cover designs:* Monica Crigler

*Website developer:* Nicole Russell

*Manufacturing:* Steve Bernier

Printed in the United States of America on acid-free paper

16  15  14        VP        3  4  5

# Contents

# Acknowledgments

I would like to thank the numerous students, parents, teachers, school districts, and research assistants who participated in the CBA project.

I especially want to thank Kathy Battista, who has provided invaluable advice and work throughout the CBA project.

Research and development of CBA was supported in part by the National Science Foundation under Grant numbers 0099047, 0352898, 554470, 838137. The opinions, findings, conclusions, and recommendations, however, are those of the author and do not necessarily reflect the views of the National Science Foundation.

—*Michael Battista*

# Introduction

Traditional mathematics instruction requires all students to learn a fixed curriculum at the same pace and in the same way. At any point in traditional curricula, instruction *assumes* that students have already mastered earlier content and, based on that assumption, specifies what and how students should learn next. The sequence of lessons is fixed; there is little flexibility to meet individual students' learning needs. Although this approach appears to work for the top 20 percent of students, it does not work for the other 80 percent (Battista 1999, 2001). And even for the top 20 percent of students, the traditional approach is not maximally effective (Battista 1999, 2001). For many students, traditional instruction is so distant from their needs that each day they make little or no learning progress and fall farther and farther behind curriculum demands. In contrast, Cognition-Based Assessment (CBA) offers a cognition-based framework to support teaching that enables ALL students to understand, make personal sense of, and become proficient with mathematics.

The CBA approach to teaching mathematics focuses on deep understanding and reasoning, within the context of continually assessing and understanding students' mathematical thinking, then building on that thinking instructionally. Rather than teaching predetermined, fixed content at times when it is inaccessible to many students, the CBA approach focuses on maximizing *individual student progress, no matter where students are in their personal development*. As a result, you can move your students toward reasonable, grade-level learning benchmarks in maximally effective ways. Designed to work with any curriculum, CBA will enable you to better understand and respond to your students' learning needs and help you choose instructional activities that are best for your students.

There are six books in the CBA project:

- *Cognition-Based Assessment and Teaching of Place Value*
- *Cognition-Based Assessment and Teaching of Addition and Subtraction*
- *Cognition-Based Assessment and Teaching of Multiplication and Division*
- *Cognition-Based Assessment and Teaching of Fractions*
- *Cognition-Based Assessment and Teaching of Geometric Shapes*
- *Cognition-Based Assessment and Teaching of Geometric Measurement*

Any of these books can be used independently, although you may find it helpful to refer to several because the topics covered are interrelated.

## Critical Components of CBA

The CBA approach emphasizes three key components that support students' mathematical sense making and proficiency:

- clear, coherent, and organized research-based descriptions of students' development of meaning for core ideas and reasoning processes in elementary school mathematics;
- assessment tasks that determine how each student is reasoning about these ideas; and
- detailed descriptions of the kinds of instructional activities that will help students at each level of reasoning about these ideas.

More specifically, CBA includes the following essential components.

## Levels of Sophistication in Student Reasoning

For many mathematical topics, researchers have found that students' development of mathematical conceptualizations and reasoning can be characterized in terms of "levels of sophistication" (Battista 2004; Battista & Clements 1996; Battista et al. 1998; Carpenter & Moser 1984; Cobb & Wheatley 1988; Fuson et al. 1997; Steffe 1988, 1992; van Hiele 1986). Chapter 2 describes a framework that explains the development of students' thinking and learning about place value in terms of such levels. This framework describes the "cognitive terrain" in which students' learning trajectories occur, including:

- the levels of sophistication students pass through in moving from their intuitive ideas and reasoning to a more formal understanding of mathematical concepts;
- cognitive obstacles that students face in learning; and
- fundamental mental processes that underlie concept development and reasoning.

Figure 1 sketches the cognitive terrain that students must ascend to attain understanding of place value. This terrain starts with students' preinstructional reasoning about place value, ends with a formal and deep understanding of place value, and indicates the cognitive plateaus reached by students along the way. Not pictured in the sketch are sublevels of understanding that may exist at each plateau level. Note that students may travel slightly different trajectories in ascending through this cognitive terrain, and they may end their trajectories at different places, depending on the curricula and teaching they experience.

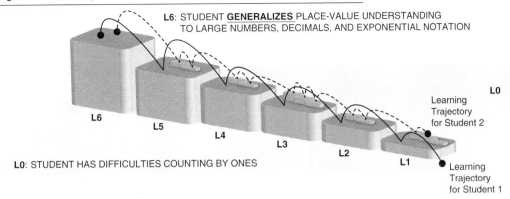

**Figure 1.** Levels of Sophistication Plateaus and Two Learning Trajectories for Place Value

## A Note About the Student Work Samples

Chapter 2 includes many examples of students' work, which are invaluable for understanding and using the levels. All of these examples are important because they show the rich diversity of student thinking at each level. However, the first time you work through the materials, you may want to read only a few examples for each type of reasoning—just enough examples to comprehend the basic idea of the level. Later, as you use the assessment tasks and instructional activities with your students, you can sharpen your understanding by examining additional examples both in the level descriptions and in the level examples for each assessment task.

## Assessment Tasks

The Appendix contains a set of CBA assessment tasks that will enable you to determine your students' mathematical thinking and precisely locate students' positions in the cognitive terrain for learning that idea. These tasks not only assess exactly what students can do, they reveal students' reasoning and underlying mathematical cognitions. The tasks are followed by a description of what each level of reasoning might look like for each assessment task. These descriptions will help you pinpoint your students' positions in the cognitive terrain of learning.

Using CBA assessment tasks to determine which levels of sophistication students are using will help you pinpoint students' learning progress, know where students should proceed next in constructing meaning and competence for the idea, and decide which instructional activities will best promote students' movement to higher levels of reasoning. It can also help guide your questions and responses in classroom discussions and in students' small-group work. The CBA website at www.heinemann .com/products/E04343.aspx includes additional assessment tasks that you can use to further investigate your students' understanding of place value.

## Instructional Suggestions

Chapter 3 provides suggestions for instructional activities that can help students progress to higher levels of reasoning. These activities are designed to meet the needs of students at each CBA level. The instructional suggestions are not meant to be comprehensive treatments of topics. Instead, they are intended to help you understand what kinds of tasks may help students make progress from one level or sublevel to the next higher level or sublevel.

## Using the CBA Materials

## Determining Students' Levels of Sophistication

There are several ways to use CBA assessment tasks to determine students' levels of sophistication in reasoning about place value.

### Individual Interviews

The most accurate way to determine students' levels of sophistication is to administer the CBA assessment tasks in individual interviews with students.[1] For many students, interviews make describing their thinking much easier—they are perfectly capable of describing their thinking orally but have difficulty doing it in writing. Individual interviews also enable teachers to ask probing questions at just the right time, which can be extremely helpful in revealing students' thinking. (Beyond assessment purposes, the individual attention students receive in individual assessment interviews provides students with added motivation, engagement, and learning.)

### Whole-Class Discussion

In an "embedded assessment" model—in which assessment is embedded within instruction—you can give an assessment task to your whole class as an instructional activity. Each student should have a student sheet with the task on it. Students do all their work on their student sheets and describe in writing how they solve the task. When all the students are done writing descriptions of their solution methods, have a class discussion of those methods. For instance, many teachers have a number of individual students present their solutions on an overhead projector or a document-projection device. As students describe their thinking, ask questions that encourage students to provide the detail you need to be able to determine what levels of reasoning they are using. Also, at times, you can repeat, paraphrase, or summarize students' thinking in ways that model good explanations (but be sure to provide accurate descriptions of what students say rather than formal versions of their reasoning). After each different student explanation, ask how many students

---

[1] For helpful advice on scheduling and conducting student interviews, see Buschman (2001).

used the strategy described. It is important that you not only have students orally describe their solution strategies but that you talk about how they can write and represent their strategies on paper. For instance, after a student has orally described his strategy, ask the class, "How could you describe this strategy on paper so I would understand it without being able to talk to you?"

Another way to see if students' written descriptions accurately describe their solution strategies is to ask students to come up to your desk and tell you individually what they did, which you can then compare to what they wrote.

## Individual and Small-Group Work

You can determine the nature of students' reasoning by circulating around the room as students are working individually or in small groups on CBA assessment tasks or instructional activities. Observe student strategies and ask students to describe what they are doing as they are doing it. Seeing students actually work on problems often provides more accurate insights into what they are doing and thinking than merely hearing explanations of their completed solutions (which sometimes do not match what they did). Also, as you talk to and observe students during individual or small-group problem solving, for students who are having difficulty accurately describing their work, write notes to yourself on students' papers that tell you what they said and did (these notes are descriptive, not evaluative).

## The Importance of Questioning

Keep in mind that the more students describe their thinking, the better they will become at describing that thinking, especially if you guide them toward providing increasingly accurate and detailed descriptions of their reasoning. For instance, if a student says, "I counted," ask, "How did you count? Count out loud to show me what you did. How could you write about what you did?"

As a more specific example, consider a student working on the problem, "Mary has 35 apples and Liz has 27 apples. How many apples do they have altogether?" Suppose Jim writes "35 + 27 = 62" as his explanation of his strategy. Ask additional questions.

**Teacher:** *What did you do to figure out that 35 + 27 = 62?*

**Jim:** *I counted.*

**Teacher:** *How did you count—count out loud for me.*

**Jim:** *35, 45, 55, 60, 62.*

**Teacher:** *Okay, that's a great way to solve the problem. How could we write that on your sheet?*

**Jim:** *I wrote that I counted.*

**Teacher:** *Great. And what else could you write so I know how you counted?*

**Jim:** *I don't know.*

**Teacher:** *What numbers did you say when you counted?*

**Jim:** *35, 45, 55, 60, 62.*

**Teacher:** *So, you could write these numbers on your sheet.*

Here are some questions that can be helpful in conducting individual interviews, interacting with students during small-group work, or conducting a classroom discussion of an assessment task:

- That's interesting; tell me what you did.
- Tell me how you found your answer.
- How did you figure out this problem?
- I'd really like to understand how you're thinking; can you tell me more about it?
- Why did you do that?
- What were you thinking when you moved these objects?
- Did you check your answer to see whether it is correct? How?
- Explain your drawing to me.
- What do these marks that you made mean?
- What were you thinking when you did this part of the problem?
- What do you mean when you say . . . ?

## Monitoring the Development of Students' Reasoning

The CBA materials are designed to help you assess levels of reasoning, not levels of students. Indeed, a student might use different levels of reasoning on different tasks. For instance, a student might operate at a higher level when using physical materials such as place-value blocks than when she does not have physical materials to support her thinking. Also, a student might operate at different levels on tasks that are familiar to her, or that she has practiced, as opposed to tasks that are totally new to her. So, rather than attempting to assign a single level to a student, you should analyze a student's reasoning on several assessment tasks, then develop an overall profile of how she is reasoning about the topic. An example of how this is done is given in Chapter 2.

To carefully monitor and even report to parents the development of student reasoning about particular mathematical topics, many teachers keep detailed records of students' CBA reasoning levels during the school year. To do this, choose several CBA assessment tasks for each major mathematical topic you will cover during the year. Administer these tasks to all of your students either as individual interviews or as written work at several different times during the school year (say before and after each curriculum unit dealing with the topic). In addition to noting the tasks used and the date, record what levels each student used on the tasks.

# Differentiating Instruction to Meet Individual Students' Learning Needs

You can tailor instruction to meet individual students' learning needs in several ways.

## Individualized Instruction

The most effective way to meet students' learning needs is to work with them individually, using the levels and tasks to precisely assess and guide students' learning. This approach is an extremely powerful way to maximize an individual student's learning.

## Instruction by CBA Groups

Another effective way of meeting students' needs is putting students into groups based on their CBA levels of reasoning about a mathematical topic. You can then look to the instructional suggestions for tasks that will be maximally effective for helping the students in each group. For instance, you might have three or four groups in your class, each consisting of students who are reasoning at about the same CBA levels and need the same type of instruction.

## Whole-Class Instruction

Another approach that many teachers have used successfully is selecting sets of tasks that all students in a class can benefit from doing. You do this by first determining the different levels of reasoning among students in the class. Then, as you consider possible instructional tasks, ask yourself:

- "How will students at each level of reasoning attempt to do this task?"
- "Can students at different levels of reasoning *succeed* on the task by using different strategies?" (Avoid tasks that some students will not have any way of completing successfully.)
- "How will students at each level benefit by doing the task?"
- "Will seeing how different students do the task help other students progress to higher levels of thinking because they are ready to hear new ways of reasoning about the task?"

Also, sets of tasks can be sequenced so that initial problems target students using lower levels of reasoning whereas later tasks target students using higher levels.

Another way to individualize whole-class instruction is to ask different questions to students at different levels as you circulate among students working in small groups. For instance, for students who are operating on numbers as collections of ones, you might ask if there is another way to count to solve the problem—can they use skip-counting? On the same problem, for students who are already skip-counting, you might ask students if they can do the problem without counting (say, by using number properties and derived facts). Knowledge of CBA levels is invaluable in devising good questions, and in asking appropriate questions for different students. In fact, when preparing to teach a lesson, many teachers use levels-of-sophistication descriptions to think about the kinds of questions they will ask students who are functioning at different levels.

Choosing which students to put into small groups for whole-class inquiry-based instruction is also important. If you think of your students' CBA levels of reasoning on a particular type of task as being divided into three groups, you might put students in the high and middle groups together, or students in the middle and low groups together. Generally, putting students in the high and low groups together is not effective because their thinking is likely to be too different.

## Assessment and Accountability

As a consequence of state and federal testing and accountability initiatives, most school districts and teachers are looking for materials and methods that will help them achieve state performance benchmarks. CBA is a powerful tool that can help you help your students achieve these benchmarks by:

▦ monitoring students' development of reasoning about core mathematical ideas;

▦ identifying students who are having difficulties learning these ideas and diagnosing the nature of these difficulties;

▦ understanding the nature of weaknesses identified by annual state mathematics assessments results *along with causes for these weaknesses*; and

▦ understanding a framework for remediating student difficulties in conceptually and cognitively sound ways.

## Moving Beyond Deficit Models

The CBA materials can help you move beyond the "deficit" model of traditional diagnosis and remediation. In the deficit model, teachers wait until students fail before attempting to diagnose and remediate their learning problems. CBA offers a more powerful, preventative model for helping students. By using CBA materials to appropriately pretest students on core ideas that are needed for upcoming instructional units, you can identify which students need help and the nature of the help they need before they fail. By then using appropriate instructional activities, you can help students acquire the core knowledge needed to be successful in the upcoming units—making that instruction effective rather than ineffective for these students.

## The Research Base

Not only have these materials gone through extensive field testing with both students and teachers, the CBA approach is consistent with major scientific theories describing how students learn mathematics *with understanding*. These theories agree that mathematical ideas must be personally constructed by students as they intentionally try to make sense of situations, and that to be effective, mathematics teaching must carefully guide and support students' construction of personally meaningful mathematical ideas (Baroody & Ginsburg, 1990; Battista, 1999, 2001; Bransford, Brown, & Cocking, 1999; De Corte, Greer, & Verschaffel, 1996; Greeno, Collins, & Resnick, 1996; Hiebert & Carpenter, 1992; Lester, 1994; National Research Council 1989; Prawat, 1999; Romberg, 1992; Schoenfeld, 1994; Steffe & Kieren, 1994; von Glasersfeld, 1995). Research shows that when students' current ideas and beliefs are ignored, their development of mathematical understanding suffers. And conversely, "There is a good deal of evidence that learning is enhanced when teachers pay attention to the knowledge and beliefs that learners bring to a learning task, use this knowledge as a starting point for new instruction, and monitor students' changing conceptions as instruction proceeds" (Bransford, et al., 1999, p. 11).

The CBA approach is also consistent with research on mathematics teaching. For instance, based on their research in the Cognitively Guided Instruction program, Carpenter and Fennema concluded that teachers must "have an understanding of the general stages that students pass through in acquiring the concepts and procedures in the domain, the processes that are used to solve different problems at each stage, and the nature of the knowledge that underlies these processes" (1991, p. 11). Indeed, a number of studies have shown that when teachers learn about such research on students' mathematical thinking, they can use that knowledge in ways that have a positive impact on their students' mathematics learning (Carpenter et al., 1998; Cobb et al., 1991; Fennema & Franke, 1992; Fennema et al., 1996; Steff & D'Ambrosio, 1995). These materials will enable you to:

- develop a detailed understanding of your students' current reasoning about specific mathematical topics, and
- choose learning goals and instructional activities to help your students build on their current ways of reasoning.

Indeed, these materials provide the kind of coherent, detailed, and well-organized research-based knowledge about students' mathematical thinking that research has indicated is important for teaching (Fennema & Franke, 1992).

Research also shows that using formative assessment can produce significant learning gains in all students (Black & Wiliam, 1998). Furthermore, formative assessment can be especially helpful for struggling students, so it can reduce achievement gaps in mathematics learning. The CBA materials offer teachers a powerful type of *formative assessment* that monitors students' learning in ways that enable teaching to be adapted to meet students' learning needs. "For assessment to function formatively, the results have to be used to adjust teaching and learning" (Black and William, 1998, p. 142). To implement high quality formative assessment, the major question that must be asked is, "Do I really know enough about the understanding of my pupils to be able to help each of them?" (Black and William, 1998, p. 143). CBA materials help answer this question.

## Using CBA Materials for RTI

Response to Intervention (RTI) is a school-based, tiered prevention and intervention model for helping all students learn mathematics. Tier 1 focuses on high-quality classroom instruction for all students. Tier 2 focuses on supplemental, differentiated instruction to address particular needs of students within the classroom context. Tier 3 focuses on intensive individualized instruction for students who are not making adequate progress in Tiers 1 and 2.

CBA can be effectively used for all three RTI tiers. For Tier 1, CBA materials provide extensive, research-based descriptions of the development of students' learning of particular mathematical topics. Research shows that teachers who understand such information about student learning teach in ways that produce greater student achievement. For Tier 2, CBA descriptions enable you to better understand and monitor each student's mathematics learning through observation, embedded assessment, questioning, informal assessment during small-group work, and formal assessment. You can then choose instructional activities that meet your students' learning needs—whole-class tasks that benefit students at all levels; different tasks for small groups of students at the same levels; individualized supplementary student work. For Tier 3, CBA assessments and level-specific instructional suggestions provide road maps and directions for giving struggling students the long-term individualized instruction sequences they need.

## Supporting Students' Development of Mathematical Reasoning

CBA materials are designed to help students move to higher levels of reasoning. It is important, however, that instruction not *demand* that students "move up" the levels with insufficient cognitive support. Such demands result in students rotely memorizing procedures that they cannot make personal sense of. *Jumps in levels are made internally by students, not by teachers or the curriculum.* This does not mean that students must progress through the levels with no help. Teaching helps students by providing them with the right kinds of encouragement, support, and challenges—having students work on problems that stretch but do not overwhelm their reasoning, asking good questions, having them discuss their ideas with other students, and sometimes showing them ideas that they don't invent themselves. When we show students ideas, we should not demand that they use them. Instead, we should try to get students to adopt new ideas because they make personal sense of the ideas and see the new ideas as better than the ideas they currently use.

# Chapter 1

## Introduction to Understanding Place Value

Once students develop an initial understanding of whole numbers and counting, they should move toward understanding the place-value concepts in our numeration system. In that system, the value of a digit depends on its location, or *place*, in the written numeral. To fully understand what written numerals mean—and to use them in counting and arithmetic operations—students must understand how our numeration system assigns values to the different places, or digits, in written numerals, and they must understand the system of words used to refer to numbers. For example, for the number 23; students must understand the words used to refer to 23 (twenty-three), and that the 2 means 2 tens (which equals 20 ones), and the 3 means 3 ones.

## Place Value: The Mathematical Perspective

Because the values of the places for digits in our place-value system are based on powers of ten, it is often called a base-ten numeration system. According to this system, the value of the number 5634.792 is determined by the values of the places of its digits, each value being based on a different power of ten, as shown in the following chart.

| $10^3 = 10 \times 10 \times 10$ | $10^2 = 10 \times 10$ | $10^1 = 10$ | $10^0 = 1$ | | $1/10^1 = 1/10$ | $1/10^2 = 1/(10 \times 10)$ | $1/10^3 = 1/(10 \times 10 \times 10)$ |
|---|---|---|---|---|---|---|---|
| thousands | hundreds | tens | ones | . | tenths | hundredths | thousandths |
| 5 | 6 | 3 | 4 | . | 7 | 9 | 2 |

The name for the number represented by the written numeral 5634.792 is "five thousand, six hundred, thirty-four and seven hundred ninety-two thousandths," which can be written as a sum of its *place-value parts* in various ways:

$$5634.792 = 5 \text{ thousands} + 6 \text{ hundreds} + 3 \text{ tens} + 4 \text{ ones} + 7 \text{ tenths} + 9 \text{ hundredths} + 2 \text{ thousandths};$$

$$= 5000 + 600 + 30 + 4 + \frac{7}{10} + \frac{9}{100} + \frac{2}{1000}$$

$$= (5 \times 1000) + (6 \times 100) + (3 \times 10) + (4 \times 1) + \left(7 \times \frac{1}{10}\right) + \left(9 \times \frac{1}{100}\right) + \left(2 \times \frac{1}{1000}\right)$$

$$= 5(10^3) + 6(10^2) + 3(10^1) + 4(10^0) + 7(10^{-1}) + 9(10^{-2}) + 2(10^{-3})$$

This base-ten scheme extends infinitely in both directions, to the left and right of the decimal point.

## Place Value: The Student Perspective

This CBA book describes two interrelated components of students' understanding of place value:

1. understanding place value in individual numbers, and

2. understanding place value in computational algorithms[1] for arithmetic (addition, subtraction, multiplication, and division of multidigit numbers).

---

[1]For this discussion, a computational algorithm is a precisely specified sequence of steps that produces an answer to a multidigit problem in whole-number addition, subtraction, multiplication, or division.

## Understanding Place Value in Individual Numbers

Before students attempt to understand place value, they must first understand whole numbers (1, 2, 3, and so on) as telling how many objects are in a set. And they must understand counting as setting up a one-to-one correspondence between a sequence of counting words (*one*, *two*, *three*, and so on) and the objects in the set. Of course, students generally do not explicitly think of counting in terms of one-to-one correspondences; instead, they attend to this reasoning implicitly when they make sure that each object is counted once and only once.

Counting is the foundation for the development of students' understanding of number. Students count by ones to determine the number of objects in a set or group. They use skip-counting to shorten the counting-by-ones process. They skip-count by place values—tens, hundreds, thousands—to develop initial understanding of place value. For instance, initially, when asked how many tens are in 43, many students count 10, 20, 30, 40 while raising 4 fingers; because 4 fingers are raised, there are 4 tens in 40.

Gradually, as students develop more sophisticated ideas about place value, they replace counting procedures with procedures for combining and separating numbers by place-value parts. But even these more sophisticated procedures can be traced to meanings given to numbers by counting. For instance, students might say that 40 plus 30 equals 70 because they can count on 30 by tens, 40, 50, 60, 70. Or students might say that 40 plus 30 equals 70 because 4 tens plus 3 tens equals 7 tens, and 7 tens is 70 because if they count by ten 7 times, they get 70.

## Understanding Place Value in Computational Algorithms

Understanding common computational algorithms for whole-number arithmetic requires students to understand place value and properties of numbers. For example, adding multidigit numbers requires that the numbers be decomposed into their place-value parts (ones, tens, hundreds) and that these parts be manipulated according to the associative and commutative properties, as illustrated below:

$$342 + 435 = (300 + 40 + 2) + (400 + 30 + 5)$$
$$= (300 + 400) + (40 + 30) + (2 + 5)$$
$$= 700 + 70 + 7$$
$$= 777$$

Similarly, understanding common computational algorithms for multiplying multidigit numbers requires students to understand how numbers can be decomposed into their place-value parts (ones, tens, hundreds) and how these parts can be manipulated according to the distributive and commutative properties:

$$53 \times 24 = (50 + 3) \times (20 + 4)$$
$$= [(50 \times 20) + (3 \times 20)] + [(50 \times 4) + (3 \times 4)]$$
$$= (50 \times 20) + (3 \times 20) + (50 \times 4) + (3 \times 4)$$
$$= 1000 + 200 + 60 + 12$$
$$= 1272$$

Students develop conceptual understanding of computational algorithms when their understandings of place value and properties of numbers become sophisticated enough to guide and make sense of the sequence of steps in these algorithms. However, students generally do not understand this sequence of steps in the detailed way it is presented above—they simply learn to manipulate numbers in ways that are consistent with place-value decompositions and properties of numbers. For instance, students understand intuitively that to multiply $53 \times 24$ they should add the products $50 \times 20$, $50 \times 4$, $3 \times 20$, and $3 \times 4$ without understanding the algebraic properties that justify each step. Once students intuitively understand this decomposition idea, writing out the decomposition as above can help students start developing an algebraic understanding of decomposition.

## Place Value in Traditional Computational Algorithms: Hidden Meanings

The major reason traditional computational algorithms are difficult for students to make sense of—and the primary cause for many procedural errors with these algorithms—is that place-value ideas are often "hidden." And just how hidden these ideas are depends on the language students use while performing the procedures.

For instance, consider how the "1" is used in traditional Algorithms A and B below. In Algorithm A, the student takes 1 from 4 and places it next to the 6—the place-value ideas that underlie these digit manipulations are hidden by both the symbols and the language. In Algorithm B, the student subtracts 1 ten from 4 tens and adds it to 6 to make 16. The language and symbol manipulation make the steps in Algorithm B meaningful in terms of properties of numbers and place value. As another example, in Algorithm C, Student 1 uses language that suggests little understanding of place value whereas Student 2 uses language suggesting a strong understanding of underlying place-value ideas. Thus the words that students use when performing algorithms can be critical to their understanding of the algorithms, and to your understanding of their understanding. Keep in mind, however, that some students will use the shorthand language of Algorithm A but still be able to explain what is meant in terms of place value *if asked*.

| Algorithm A | Algorithm B | Algorithm C |
|---|---|---|
| $\overset{3}{\cancel{4}}\overset{1}{6}$ <br> $-17$ <br> $\overline{\phantom{0}29}$ | $\overset{3}{\cancel{4}}\overset{16}{\cancel{6}}$ <br> $-17$ <br> $\overline{\phantom{0}29}$ | $\overset{1}{46}$ <br> $+17$ <br> $\overline{\phantom{0}63}$ |
| **S:** Take 1 from the 4 and put it with the 6. | **S:** Take 1 ten from the 4 tens and add it to the 6 to make 16. | **S1:** 6 plus 7 equals 13. Put down the 3 carry the 1. 1 plus 4 plus 1 equals 6, put down the 6. <br><br> **S2:** 6 plus 7 equals 13. Put down the 3 and bring 1 ten over to the tens column. 1 ten plus 4 tens plus 1 ten equals 6 tens, write 6 in the tens column. |

Importantly, place-value understanding can help students make sense of subtle but critical ideas in these algorithms—ideas that cause difficulties for many students. For instance, in Algorithm A, why is the 1 put next to the 6 to create 16, whereas in Algorithm C, the 1 is added to the 4? Using Algorithm B and Student 2's description of Algorithm C can help students answer this question—and thus make sense of the mathematics.

## Relating Place Value in Numbers and Place Value in Algorithms

This CBA book describes levels of sophistication in elementary students' development of understanding of place value, both in numbers and in algorithms. (Further discussion of place-value understanding with operations and algorithms is given in the *Cognition-Based Assessment and Teaching of Addition and Subtraction* and *Cognition-Based Assessment and Teaching of Multiplication and Division* books.)

The Place-Value Levels chart on page 7 provides an overview of how students' development of understanding of place value in numbers and algorithms are related. *In the CBA recommended sequence of development, students fully achieve Level 3 reasoning before they are introduced to any type of algorithm.* Then they are introduced to the expanded algorithm (Level 4), followed by the traditional algorithm (Level 5). Learning addition and subtraction algorithms should precede learning multiplication and division algorithms.

The recommended sequence of development is rarely achieved in schools. Often students are introduced (by curricula or parents) to algorithms much too early in their development of understanding of place value. The chart makes clear that if algorithms are introduced prematurely (when students are still thinking of numbers in terms of *counting* by ones or even tens), students learn the algorithms rotely (if at all). Premature focus on algorithms also curtails students' development of understanding of place value, with students stagnating at Level 1.

## Important Comment on Counting Words Versus Objects

At each level, counting physical or visual objects is less sophisticated than counting "counting words" or even counting fingers. For example, suppose a student is asked what must be added to 7 to get 12, and counts 8, 9, 10, 11, 12, raising one finger after each count, then says 5. In this case, the student has counted the counting words 8, 9, 10, 11, 12 by raising his fingers then recognizing the finger pattern for 5. More sophisticated reasoning would be the dual counting procedure, "8 is 1, 9 is 2, 10 is 3, 11 is 4, 12 is 5." Counting fingers is more sophisticated than counting given objects because when counting fingers, students must "produce" fingers and consider them as countable, whereas when counting given objects, the objects are already "out there" to be counted.

Because counting just count words is more abstract than counting fingers, which is slightly more abstract than counting objects, we should always determine if students need visible or physical materials to implement their reasoning. So, for instance, if a task does not provide these materials and students ask for them, ask students if they can do the problem without the materials. Then let them check their answers with the materials. (But if they cannot do the task without materials, give them materials.) Similarly, students often use a more sophisticated level of reasoning when they can manipulate place-value blocks than when no blocks or pictures of blocks are available. So, when determining students' CBA levels of reasoning, it is important to know what kinds of materials students need to implement the level.

## Understanding Students' Levels of Sophistication for Place Value

The CBA approach to helping students understand place value is built around detailed descriptions of levels of reasoning that allow us to tailor our instruction to meet students' learning needs. At first glance, the amount of detail can be overwhelming. So, keep in mind that understanding CBA levels develops in stages and over time. First, focus on learning the major features of the levels. Then, as you use CBA with your students, you will learn the finer details of the CBA framework.

### Zooming Out to Get an Overview

To get an idea of the overall organization of the levels, examine the following "zoomed out" view of the major ways students think about place value. Familiarize yourself with these major levels first, without worrying about the sublevels that are discussed in Chapter 2.

| Place-Value Levels: Zoomed Out to Major Levels | | |
|---|---|---|
| **Level 0** | **Student has difficulties counting by ones.** | *No use of algorithms* |
| **Level 1** | **Student operates on numbers as <u>collections of ones</u> (no skip-counting by place value).** | *No use or rote use of algorithms* |
| **Level 2** | **Student operates on numbers by <u>skip-counting</u> by place value (e.g., counts by tens).** | *No use or use of algorithms with weak or no connection between place value and algorithms* |
| **Level 3** | **Student operates on numbers by <u>combining</u> and <u>separating</u> place-value parts (e.g., adds tens parts without counting).** | *Explicit use of place value in informal multidigit arithmetic; emerging but incomplete understanding of place value in algorithms* |
| **Level 4** | **Student understands place value in expanded algorithms.** | *Place-value understanding of expanded algorithms (through hundreds)* |
| **Level 5** | **Student understands place value in traditional algorithms.** | *Place-value understanding of traditional algorithms (through hundreds)* |
| **Level 6** | **Student generalizes place-value understanding to large numbers, numbers less than 1, and exponential notation.** | *Place-value understanding of algorithms for any size numbers, including decimals* |

In the top row of this zoomed out view, Level 0, students do not understand how to count groups of objects by ones. In Levels 1 through 3, students progress from fluent counting of objects by ones, to counting by tens, then to combining tens and ones. In Level 4, students solidify their reasoning of combining numbers by place value into the structure of place-value transparent expanded algorithms. In Level 5, students understand place value in traditional algorithms, where place-value ideas are hidden. Finally, in the bottom row, Level 6, students generalize their understanding of place value to all numbers—those that are very large and those that are less than 1—and use exponential notation.

## Zooming In to Meet Individual Students' Needs

Understanding individual students' reasoning precisely enough to maximize their learning or remediate a learning difficulty requires a more detailed picture. We must "zoom in" to see sublevels (see Figure 1.1). The "jumps" between sublevels must be small enough that students can achieve them with small amounts of instruction in relatively short periods of time.

Imagine students trying to climb the plateaus in the cognitive terrain described by CBA levels. In Situation A, the student has to make a cognitive jump that is too great. In Situation B, the student can get from Level 1 to Level 2 by using accessible sublevels as stepping-stones. To provide students the instructional guidance and cognitive support they need to develop a thorough understanding of mathematical ideas, you need to understand and use the sublevels. Chapter 2 provides detailed descriptions and illustrations of all the CBA levels and sublevels for place value.

**Figure 1.1** Accessible Cognitive Jumps

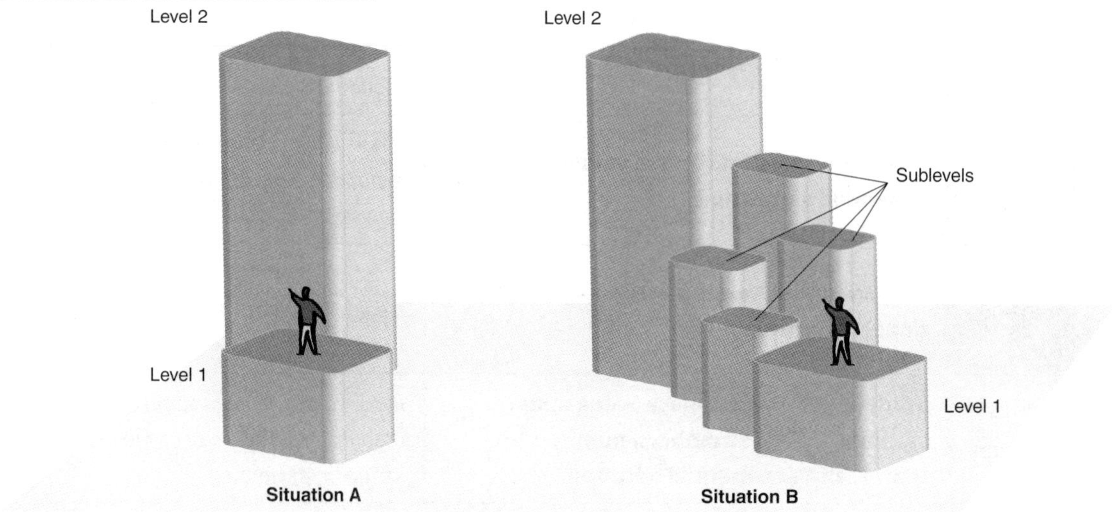

Situation A

Situation B

## Notes

1. To simplify the descriptions in this document, we often discuss only ones and tens in two-digit numbers. Similar, but more complicated, ideas occur for numbers containing more than two digits. But keep in mind that students' level of understanding of numbers with more than two digits may lag behind their level of understanding for two-digit numbers.

2. The focus of CBA is on whole-number place-value ideas and reasoning. Reasoning about operations on decimals is beyond the scope of CBA research. However, because it is very important to see how place-value ideas will mature in later grades (this is sometimes referred to as seeing the "mathematical horizon"), Level 6 describes the nature of advanced concepts of place value, including a brief discussion of decimal place value.

# Chapter 2

## Levels of Sophistication in Student Reasoning: Place Value

The CBA approach to guiding students' development of understanding of place value builds on the CBA levels of sophistication in students' reasoning. Understanding these levels allows teachers to tailor instruction to meet students' individual learning needs. The major CBA levels (Levels 0, 1, 2, 3, 4, 5, 6) provide an overview of the ways students think about place value. These levels describe how students progress from beginning understanding of number concepts to understanding our place-value numeration system to using understanding of place value to make sense of computational algorithms for addition, subtraction, multiplication, and division.

Understanding students' reasoning precisely enough to maximize their learning or remediate their learning difficulties requires a more detailed picture than that provided by the major levels. So the major levels are divided into sublevels. The "jumps" between sublevels are small enough that students can achieve them with small amounts of instruction in relatively short periods of time. Sublevels serve as accessible stepping-stones in students' development.

The chart on page 10 summarizes the CBA levels for place value. Subsequent sections in this chapter provide a detailed description of each level, along with examples of student work at each level. At first glance, the amount of detail in the CBA levels can be overwhelming. So keep in mind that understanding CBA levels develops gradually as you study examples of students' work and as you use CBA with your students.

| Level | Sublevel | Description | Page |
|:---:|:---:|:---|:---:|
| 0 | | **Student has difficulties counting by ones.** | 11 |
| 1 | | **Student operates on numbers as <u>collections of ones</u> (no skip-counting by place value).** | 12 |
| | 1.1 | Student correctly counts groups of objects by ones but cannot count groups of ten. | 12 |
| | 1.2 | Student correctly counts groups of ten. | 14 |
| | 1.3 | Student operates on tens and ones separately as ones. | 15 |
| 2 | | **Student operates on numbers by <u>skip-counting</u> by place value (e.g., counts by tens).** | 20 |
| | 2.1 | Student counts by tens and ones separately. | 20 |
| | 2.2 | Student counts by tens in mid-decades. | 23 |
| 3 | | **Student operates on numbers by <u>combining and separating</u> place-value parts (e.g., adds tens parts without counting).** | 24 |
| | 3.1 | Student uses multiples-of-ten language ("forty plus twenty equals sixty"). | 24 |
| | 3.2 | Student uses tens language ("4 tens plus 2 tens equals 6 tens"). | 26 |
| | 3.3 | Student integrates Levels 2.1, 2.2, 3.1, and 3.2. | 28 |
| 4 | | **Student understands place value in expanded algorithms.** | 29 |
| | 4.1 | Student understands place value in expanded addition and subtraction algorithms. | 30 |
| | 4.2 | Student understands place value in expanded multiplication and division algorithms. | 31 |
| 5 | | **Student understands place value in traditional algorithms.** | 34 |
| | 5.1 | Student understands place value in traditional addition and subtraction algorithms. | 35 |
| | 5.2 | Student understands place value in traditional multiplication and division algorithms. | 36 |
| 6 | | **Student generalizes place-value understanding to larger numbers, numbers less than 1, and exponential notation.** | 38 |

# LEVEL 0: Student Has Difficulties Counting by Ones

Students' attempts to count sets of objects by ones are inaccurate, often omitting or double-counting objects. During counting, students fail to structure their counting acts in a way that tags each object once and only once.

Note: Throughout this book, the term *counting* will refer to actually counting things such as checkers, fingers, or even counting words. In the process of correct and meaningful counting of things, students implicitly set up a one-to-one correspondence between a sequence of number words and the objects they are counting so that the last number they say gives the number of objects. Mere recitation of counting words, without counting anything, will be referred to as *rote verbal counting*. (If students cannot recite counting words correctly, they are still classified as Level 0.)

You can assess students' understanding of counting by asking them to collect or produce given numbers of objects. For instance, with a sufficient supply of cubes, ask: "Can you give me 5 cubes?" "Can you give me 8 cubes?" "Can you give me 14 cubes?" "Can you give me 23 cubes?"

## EXAMPLES

**Task:** *How many cubes are there?*

Double-Counting

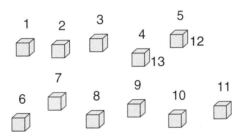

Omitting Objects in the Count

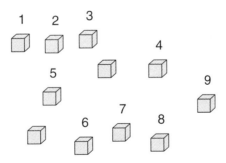

*For strategies to help students at Level 0, see Chapter 3, page 51.*

## LEVEL 1:  Student Operates on Numbers as Collections of Ones

At this level, students think of numbers only as collections of ones, and count only by ones. However, students may start to convert multiples of ten into a number of tens (e.g., thirty is 3 tens, forty is 4 tens), but they do not understand why the conversion works—it is merely a memorized rote fact. Or students might recall that digits in the same column are to be added or subtracted (but as ones), but do not understand why. Because students think of numbers as collections of ones, not in terms of their place-value parts, they cannot make place-value sense of computational algorithms, so they can learn them only by rote.

## Level 1.1  Student correctly counts groups of objects by ones but cannot count groups of ten.

Students correctly and reliably count sets of objects by ones. (Note that counting backwards is more difficult than counting forwards.) Students at this level, however, cannot conceive of groups of ten objects as countable.

### EXAMPLES

**Task:** *How many cubes are there?*

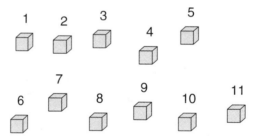

Correct counting is based on setting up a one-to-one relationship with numbers in the counting sequence, in this case 1, 2, . . . , 9, 10, 11, and the set of cubes.

**Task:** *Jon has 30 checkers. How many stacks of 10 checkers can he make?*

**Response:** *[Draws 30 circles on a piece of paper, counting by ones]* There are 30 stacks.

Cognition-Based Assessment and Teaching of Place Value

**Task:** *How many squares are there altogether?*

**Response:** *[Pointing at squares]* 1, 2, 3, 4, 5, . . . , 33, 34, 35. There's 35. *[Teacher: How many groups of ten squares are there?]* I don't know.

Even though the squares are organized into groups of ten, and even though the student has seen base-ten blocks used to represent two-digit numbers, she counts only by ones. She is unable to count groups of ten.

---

**Task:** *46 = _____ tens and _____ ones.*

**Response:** 46 equals 40 plus 6. *[Writes the following:]*

$$46 = \underline{40} \text{ tens } \textit{and} \underline{6} \text{ ones}$$

This student separated 46 into its multiples-of-ten and ones parts, but she did not understand the multiples-of-ten part in terms of groups of ten.

---

**Task:** *35 = _____ ones and _____ tens.*

**Response:** <u>3</u> ones and <u>5</u> tens.

Although this student correctly answers such problems when the answer is in the "tens, ones" order, he does this rotely, relying on order of numbers rather than an understanding of tens and ones.

---

*For strategies to help students at Level 1.1, see Chapter 3, page 53.*

# Level 1.2 Student correctly counts groups of ten.

Students can treat groups of ten ones as countable units. (Many mathematics educators call the countable groups of ten *composite units of ten* or *composites of ten*.) However, although students can count groups of ten, to find the total number of objects in several groups, *they count by ones, <u>not</u> by tens*. Students' reasoning is more sophisticated when they can count counting words instead of visible objects.

## Counting Visible Groups of Ten

Students can count groups of ten when using visible material like a picture or set of blocks.

### EXAMPLES

**Task:** *There are 43 checkers [showing randomly placed checkers on table]. How many packages of ten can I make?*

**Response:** The student rearranged the checkers as shown, counting 1 through 10 to find each group of ten. She then pointed to and counted the 4 groups of ten—1, 2, 3, 4—and said 4 (so her groups of ten were "countable").

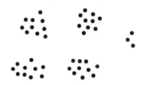

**Task:** *Roberto made 38 cookies. How many bags of 10 cookies can he make?*

**Response:** *[Using place-value blocks, counts individual one-blocks on one ten-block 1–10, counts individual one-blocks on second ten-block 11–20, counts individual one-blocks on third ten-block 21–30, counts individual one-blocks 31–38. Counts the three ten-blocks]* 1, 2, 3; 3 bags.

## Counting Groups of Counting Words

Students can count groups of ten using only counting words. This is a difficult step for many students to take because they must coordinate two simultaneous counting schemes—counting ones and counting tens.

**Task:** *47 + 27 =*

**Response:** Using her fingers, the student counted on from 47 by ones, 27 times, ending at 74. When asked how she knew to stop at 74, she said she counted 10, two times, then counted 7 more.

This student was able to count two groups of ten counting acts (using her fingers).

**Task:** *How many cubes are in 3 stacks of ten?*

**Response:** The student counted by ones, putting up one finger when she reached ten, a second finger when she reached twenty, and a third finger when she reached thirty.

This student knew that as she was counting by ones, each of the numbers 10, 20, and 30 represented an additional group of ten ones.

*For strategies to help students at Level 1.2, see Chapter 3, page 53.*

## Level 1.3  Student operates on tens and ones separately as ones.

Because of instruction on place value or algorithms, students start to see the digits in multidigit numbers as different. But they do not genuinely understand the values of digits in different places in a number. So, in adding two numbers, students treat the digits in the ones columns as one set of ones, and the digits in the tens columns as a second set of ones. Even though students sometimes use the term "tens," students treat tens and ones as unrelated objects, like apples and oranges; *they don't understand that each ten is equal to 10 ones.* If asked why they add the digits in the ones column, then the digits in the tens column, students say something like, "That's just what you are supposed to do." Students at this level cannot meaningfully explain regrouping in addition and subtraction of multidigit numbers. Students find the total value of a sum or difference by counting by ones, although they might start the count with a multiple of ten, or decade number.[1] That is, students may translate directly from number of tens (e.g., 3 tens) to counting-by-ones words (e.g., thirty), but they give no evidence that they have counted tens in doing this translation. For example, students might say that 3 tens is thirty without counting "ten, twenty, thirty" or giving any other explanation.

Because students think of numbers as collections of ones, they cannot meaningfully reason about numbers in terms of their place-value parts. So if students learn an algorithm for an arithmetic operation, they treat multidigit numbers as strings of

[1]A *multiple of ten*, or *decade number*, is a number like 10, 30, 70, or 230 because $10 = 10 \times 1, 30 = 10 \times 3, 70 = 10 \times 7, 230 = 10 \times 23.$

digits that are manipulated according to rules that are not understood. Sometimes students' use of rote algorithms is correct, but other times it is incorrect.

At this level, many students can correctly use base-ten blocks, but they do so rotely.

## EXAMPLES

**Task:** *7 + 600 + 40 =*

**Response:** *[Writes a 6]* 7 plus 4 equals 11 *[Writes 11 after the 6]* 611.

---

**Task:** *39 + 46 =*

**Response:** 3 + 4 = 7 *[Writes 7]*. 9 + 6 = 15, and I don't know if I should write the 1 or the 5. So I am going to go with the 5 because my mom told me to use the second number *[Writes 5]*. So I say 75.

---

**Task:** *Circle in the dot picture what this part of the number means [pointing to the 2 in the numeral 23].*

**Response:** *[Circles 2 dots in the group of 3]* Because these two are 2 *[pointing to the 2 dots he circled]* and this is 2 *[pointing to the 2 in 23]*.

---

**Task:** *How many squares are there altogether?*

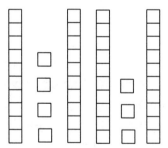

**Response:** *[Pointing at the first ten-strip from the left]* 10 *[Pointing at the next 4 individual squares]* 11, 12, 13, 14. *[Pointing at the next two ten-strips]* 15, 16. *[Pointing at the next 3 individual squares]* 17, 18, 19. *[Pointing at the last ten-strip]* 20.

This student lost track of the values of the ten-strips.

**Task:** *46 = _____ tens and _____ ones.*

**Response:** You put the 4 in the tens, and the 6 in the ones. *[Teacher: How did you know there were 4 tens?]* I just know it. I put 4 by the tens because that's what my mom told me. *[Given the problem 60 + 8 = _____ tens and _____ ones]* Add the 60 and 8 and that's 68 *[Writes 68]*. Then put 6 for the tens and 8 for the ones. *[Given 5 tens and 3 ones = _____ tens and 13 ones]*. It's 5 tens and 3 ones *[Crosses out the 1 in "13 ones"]*.

This is an example of rote conversion of numbers into tens and ones. This student translates 46 into tens and ones parts but is unable to justify this translation in terms of groups of ten or counting by tens. Importantly, she converted 60 + 8 to 68 before she could do the second problem. If she really understood tens and ones, she would have immediately seen that 60 is 6 tens. Finally, she was unable to do the third problem because she does not understand the relationship between tens and ones.

**Task:** *Roberto made 38 cookies. How many bags of 10 cookies can he make?*

**Response:** *[Uses base-ten blocks to make 38 as 3 ten-blocks and 8 one-blocks. Counts the 3 ten-blocks]* 1, 2, 3 bags. *[Teacher: How many cookies are in the 3 bags? Student counts individual one-blocks on the 3 ten-blocks:]* 1, 2, . . . , 29, 30. There's 30 cookies.

**Task:** *306 – 128 =*

**Response:** After attempting to solve the problem symbolically, the student uses place-value blocks to make 306. He decides that he needs to trade 1 hundred-block for some ten-blocks. He carefully lines up, but does not count, 9 ten-blocks under 1 hundred-block and says that it is 10 tens (the blocks are not true to size). The student then removes 1 hundred-block, 2 ten-blocks, and 6 one-blocks, and covers 2 one-blocks on one of the remaining ten-blocks. He evaluates what's left—1 hundred-block, 6 ten-blocks, and 8 ones on the ten-block in which he covered 2 ones. He gets an answer of 168.

This is an example of rote use of base-ten blocks. This student did not understand that 1 hundred equals 10 tens; his conceptualization of the relationship between tens and ones in this episode was visually based.

**Task:** *3 × 26 =*

**Response:** *[Student makes 3 sets of 2 ten-blocks and 6 one-blocks.]*

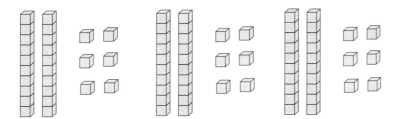

Three groups of 26. *[Counts all cubes by ones]* 1, 2, 3, . . . , 78.

**Task:** *In a box, there are 35 red apples and 27 green apples. How many apples are in the box?*

**Response:** *[Makes 35 with base-ten blocks, then 27 with base-ten blocks, and puts the ten-blocks together and one-blocks together. Lays his hand on the 5 ten-blocks.]* 50. *[Counts by ones]* 51, 52, 53, . . . , 61, 62.

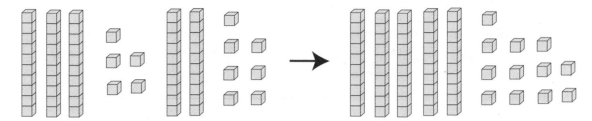

This student knew how to represent numbers with place-value blocks, but he did not perform any regrouping—he treated the numbers as collections of ones, never showing that he fully understood the connection between tens and ones.

## Rote Use of Algorithms

Students operate on numbers or perform arithmetic procedures rotely, sometimes incorrectly and sometimes correctly. The first set of examples illustrate that when students are adding or subtracting, they often regroup in ways that violate place-value concepts.

**Task:** *There are 27 squares under the mat. How many squares are there altogether?*

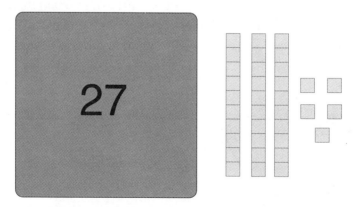

**Response:** 27 plus 35. *[Writes in vertical format and gets 512 as the answer.]*

$$\begin{array}{r} 27 \\ +\ 35 \\ \hline 512 \end{array}$$

Cognition-Based Assessment and Teaching of Place Value

**Task:** *267 + 189 =*

**Response:** *[Writes "200 + 67 + 100 + 89." She draws segments from 200 and 100 and pauses. The teacher offers her place-value blocks. Student puts out 3 hundred-blocks, then writes 300 for the sum of 100 and 200. Student then places a plus sign between the 6 and 7 in 67 and adds the two digits.]* 7 plus 6 is 13. *[Student then does the same with the 8 and 9 in 89, adds the digits, and writes 17. She then draws segments from the 13 and 17.]* 17 plus 13 equals 20 because 3 plus 7 equals 10 and 1 plus 1 equals 2. I take the zero from the 10 and I know that 1 plus 1 equals 2. *[Draws lines from 300 and 20 and writes 320.]*

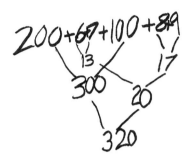

This student is trying to extend a procedure that she has used correctly for adding two-digit numbers (see the diagram below for her work in adding 35 and 27). But because her knowledge of using this procedure is not guided by a firm understanding of place value, her extension fails.

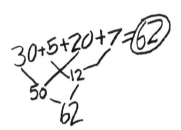

This example illustrates that students can learn even expanded algorithms rotely.

---

**Task:** *46 + 17 =*

$$\begin{array}{r} {}^{1}46 \\ +17 \\ \hline 63 \end{array}$$

**Response:** *[Writes as shown above]* 6 plus 7 equals 13. Put down the 3 carry the 1. 1 plus 4 plus 1 equals 6, put down the 6. Sixty-three. *[Teacher, pointing to the 1 above the 4: What does this mean?]* It's one. *[Teacher: Why did you put it above the 4?]* Because you're supposed to carry it over there.

This student uses the addition algorithm correctly but rotely. She still thinks of numbers strictly as collections of ones and cannot use place-value concepts to explain why what she is doing is correct. When students perform algorithms correctly, if their language does not indicate an understanding of place value, only questioning will reveal whether students understand the place-value ideas imbedded in the algorithm.

*For strategies to help students at Level 1.3, see Chapter 3, page 53.*

## LEVEL 2: Student Operates on Numbers by Skip-Counting by Place Value

At this level, students understand the connection between counting by ones (1, 2, 3, . . .) and counting by tens (10, 20, 30, . . .). They understand that each counting-by-ten act (e.g., 10, 20, 30) is equivalent to ten counting-by-ones acts. So, when appropriate in reasoning about two-digit numbers, students shorten the process of counting by ones by skip-counting by tens.

Counting by tens in mid-decades is more sophisticated than counting by tens and ones separately. That is, first, students learn to count by tens, starting with a multiple of ten; for example, 10, 20, 30 or 40, 50, 60. Later, when their reasoning becomes more sophisticated, students learn to count by tens, starting with numbers that are not multiples of ten (mid-decade numbers). For example, they count 25, 35, 45 or 47, 57, 67. Also, skip-counting strictly verbally is more sophisticated than implementing it concretely or pictorially.

If students learn algorithms at this level, they make weak or no connections between place value and the algorithms, so their learning of algorithms is rote.

## Level 2.1 Student counts by tens and ones separately.

Students add and subtract numbers by counting by tens and ones separately.

## Using Visual/Physical Material

### EXAMPLES

**Task:** *There are 27 squares under the mat. How many squares are there altogether?*

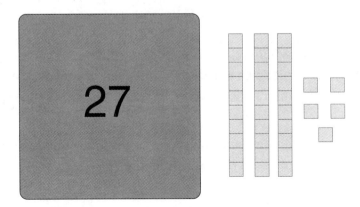

Cognition-Based Assessment and Teaching of Place Value

**Response:** *[Pointing at the mat]* 10, 20 *[pointing at the ten-strips then individual squares]* 30, 40, 50; 55 *[pointing back to the mat]* 56, 57, 58, 59, 60, 61, 62.

This student counted the tens first, then the ones, using visual materials.

---

**Task:** *A number has 13 tens and 6 ones. What is the number?*

**Response:** Well 3 tens is 30, but? *[Asks for tens-blocks, then counts out 13 tens-blocks and 6 ones]* Well, let's see, 10, 20, 30, . . . ,100, 110, 120, 130! 136.

---

**Task:** *Circle in the dot picture what this part of the number means [pointing to the 2 in the numeral 23].*

**Response:** The student counted "10, 20" as he motioned over the two "columns" of two fives. He circled the set of 20 dots, saying "The two is twenty."

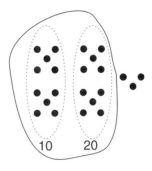

---

**Task:** *How many squares are there altogether?*

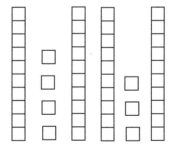

**Response:** *[Pointing at strips of ten]* 10, 20, 30, 40, *[pointing at single squares]* 41, 42, . . . , 47. *[Teacher, uncovering two additional strips: How many squares altogether if I add two more strips of ten? Student points at strips.]* 10, 20, . . . , 60; *[Pointing at singles]* 61, 62, . . . , 67.

Importantly, when the 2 additional ten-strips were added to the already-counted display, the student could not count on by tens from 47, nor did she count on by tens from 40.

**Task:** *3 × 26 =*

**Response:**

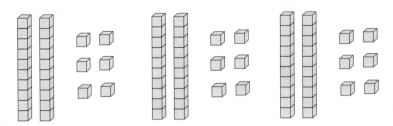

*[After making three sets of 26 with place-value blocks]* Three groups of 26. 10, 20, 30, 40, 50, 60. 6, 12, 18. 78.

## Not Using Visual/Physical Material

### EXAMPLES

**Task:** *3 × 26 =*

**Response:** Three groups of 26. 10, 20; 30, 40; 50, 60. 6, 12, 18. 78.

**Task:** *Mr. Smith has 35 candies in one hand and 24 candies in his other hand. How many candies does he have altogether?*

**Response:** *[Using fingers]* 10, 20, 30, 40, 50; 55, 56, 57, 58, 59. It's 59.

**Task:** *46 = _____ tens and _____ ones.*

**Response:** *[Counting on his fingers]* 10, 20, 30, 40 *[Writes 4 in the tens blank]* so 4 tens, and 6 ones.

**Task:** *Mary has 84 cookies. She wants to divide them equally among 4 people. How many cookies does each person get?*

**Response:** *[Writes 2 rows of 4 tens and 1 row of 4 ones; see below]* 10, 20, 30, 40, 50, 60, 70, 80; 81, 82, 83, 84. There's 4 groups *[loops 4 groups of 21]*, so each person gets 21 cookies.

```
10   10   10   10
10   10   10   10
     1 1 1 1
```
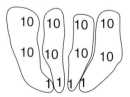

*For strategies to help students at Level 2.1, see Chapter 3, page 56.*

# Level 2.2  Student counts by tens in mid-decades.

A more sophisticated type of counting by ten occurs when students count by tens in the middle of a decade. In this type of counting, students understand and maintain the relationship between tens and ones units throughout the entire counting sequence.

## EXAMPLES

**Task:** *There are 27 squares under the mat. How many squares are there altogether?*

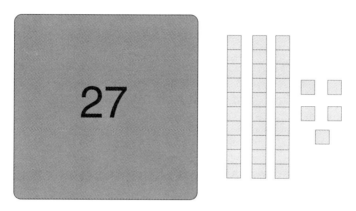

**Response 1:** *[Pointing at the ten-strips then the individual squares]* 27; 37, 47, 57; 58, 59, 60, 61, 62.

This student counts by tens starting at 27, but uses the visual material to do so.

**Response 2:** 27 *[raising 3 fingers]* 37, 47, 57 *[raising 5 fingers]* 58, 59, 60, 61, 62.

Because this student uses his fingers rather than the given pictorial material, his thinking is more sophisticated than if he had used the given pictures by pointing to them.

---

**Task:** *In a box, there are 35 red apples and 27 green apples. How many apples are in the box?*

**Response 1:** *[Sets out place-value blocks for 35 and 27, then pointing to the blocks for 35]*

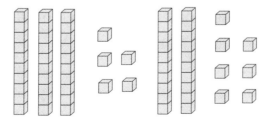

35. *[Pointing at the ten-blocks for 27]* 45, 55. *[Pointing at the one-blocks for 27]* 60; 62.

This student uses the physical/visual materials to count.

**Response 2:** *[Without using blocks]* 35, 45, 55, 60, 62.

This student's more sophisticated thinking allows him to count by tens without using materials.

---

**Task:** *40 + 8 + 20 + 7 =*

**Response:** 48, 58, 68, 70, 75.

---

**Task:** *39 plus what number equals 71?*

**Response:** 39 *[Raising 3 fingers on one hand]* 49, 59, 69. *[Raising 2 fingers on the other hand]* 70, 71. It's 32. *[Teacher: How did you get 32?]* I added ten three times and added two more.

---

*For strategies to help students at Level 2.2, see Chapter 3, page 57.*

## LEVEL 3: Student Operates on Numbers by Combining and Separating Place-Value Parts

To perform arithmetic operations, students at this level decompose numbers into their place-value parts—ones, tens, hundreds, and so on. These place-value parts are combined or separated *directly, without counting*. So, for instance, students do not count by tens. Students use either multiples-of-ten language (forty) or tens language (4 tens). For example, to find 40 + 20, students say either, "forty plus twenty equals sixty," or "4 tens plus 2 tens equals 6 tens." Because the multiples-of-ten language specifically ties units of ten to units of ones (the decade numbers 10, 20, 30 occur in the counting-by-ones sequence), it is less abstract than the tens language.

It is critical to recognize that students' reasoning about place value must be at least at Level 3 before they can truly make sense of algorithms for adding, subtracting, multiplying, and dividing whole numbers. But often, even when students do achieve Level 3 understanding, they still struggle to connect this place-value reasoning to computational algorithms, especially to traditional algorithms.

## Level 3.1  Student uses multiples-of-ten language ("forty plus twenty equals sixty").

Students combine and separate collections of tens using multiples-of-ten language. For example, a student might say, "thirty plus forty equals seventy." As students operate on composites of ten, they maintain the connection between the tens and the ones within the tens. Numbers expressed in tens language (4 tens) are translated to multiples-of-ten language (forty) before operating on them. (At the more advanced Level 3.2, students do not need to do this translation.)

**Task:** *In a box, there are 35 red apples and 27 green apples. How many apples are in the box?*

**Response 1:** 30 plus 20 is 50. And then add the 7 and 5, equals 12. So 50 and 12 is 62.

**Response 2:** 35 plus 20 is 55; plus 5 is 60, plus 2 is 62.

---

**Task:** *324 + 235 =*

**Response 1:** 300 and 200 is 500. 30 and 20 is 50; 550. And 4 and 5 is 9, so 559.

**Response 2:** 559. *[Performing the traditional algorithm but in horizontal format]* 5 + 4 = 9 so put the 9 down; 20 + 30 = 50, so put the 5 down; 300 + 200 = 500, so put the 5 down.

---

**Task:** *5 tens and 3 ones = _____ tens and 13 ones.*

**Response:** Four tens, that's 40, and if you add the ten from 13, that's 50, and then add that 3, that's 53. That would be the same as these two right here *[pointing to "5 tens and 3 ones"]*, it's 4 tens.

---

**Task:** *A number has 14 ones and 3 tens. What is the number?*

**Response:** 44. Three tens plus another ten from the 14 is 40, plus the 4 is 44.

Because the problem is posed in tens-units language, and because when the student adds "another ten" to three tens he expresses the sum in multiples-of-ten language (forty), he is classified as using multiples of ten. (When both tens-units and multiples-of-ten language are used, and it is not clear whether the student is at Levels 3.1 or 3.2, we choose 3.1 because it is the less sophisticated level and more likely to come first in students' development.)

---

**Task:** *A number has 13 tens and 6 ones. What is the number?*

**Response:** 136. Ten tens is 100, 3 tens is 30, and 6 ones; add them all together.

This student translates the tens units of the original problem to multiples-of-ten language before operating on the numbers.

---

**Task:** *85 = 7 tens and _____ ones.*

**Response:** *[Writes 15]* That *[pointing to 7 tens]* would be a 70 because it's 7 tens. Plus ten *[pointing to the 1 in his written 15]* would make the 70 an 80 and plus 5 would make 85.

**Task:** *(7 tens and 16 ones) – (5 tens and 9 ones) =*

**Response:** 70 minus 50 equals 20; 16 minus 9 is 7; 20 plus 7 is 27.

In the last two problems, the students converted numbers from tens language to multiples-of-ten language, a clear indicator of Level 3.1 reasoning.

---

**Task:** *20 × 8 =*

**Response 1:** *[Writes 160]* I know that 20 plus 20 is 40, and I add two 40s together and I get 80, then I add two 80s together and get 160. I know that 40 is two 20s; 80 is four 20s, and 160 is eight 20s.

**Response 2:** I know that 20 times 8 equals 160 because 2 times 8 is 16 and you add a zero.

---

**Task:** *43 × 20 =*

**Response:** 40 times 20 is 800. 3 times 20 is 60. 800 plus 60 equals 860.

---

*For strategies to help students at Level 3.1, see Chapter 3, page 58.*

---

## Level 3.2  Student uses tens language ("4 tens plus 2 tens equals 6 tens").

Students operate on collections of tens using tens language (3 tens plus 4 tens equals 7 tens) or hundreds language (3 hundreds plus 4 hundreds equals 7 hundreds). As students operate on tens, they maintain the connection between the tens and the ones within the tens.

Note that for 243, many students understand the wording "2 groups of one hundred, 4 groups of ten, 3 ones" before they understand the more abstract language "2 hundreds, 4 tens, 3 ones." Also, at this level students know basic relationships between place values, for example, that 1 hundred equals 10 tens. However, they justify such relationships by counting (e.g., 1 hundred equals 10 tens because if you count ten 10 times, you get 100; 10, 20, . . . , 90, 100).

**Task:** *There are 27 squares under the mat. How many squares are there altogether?*

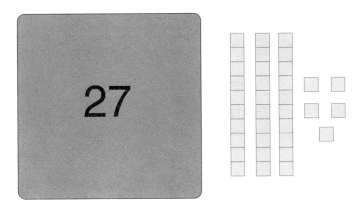

**Response:** 3 tens plus 2 more tens from the 27 is 5 tens; 7 plus 5 is one more ten, so 6 tens, and 2. So 62.

---

**Task:** *46 = _____ tens and _____ ones.*

**Response:** 4 and 6. Because this 4 [in 46] stands for tens and this 6 [in 46] stands for ones.

This explanation suggests that the student understands that the 4 in 46 means 4 tens and the 6 means 6 ones. However, students might say something like this based on rote memory (see the examples for Level 1.1). Problems like those that follow can help distinguish rote memory from an appropriate conceptualization of place value.

---

**Task:** *A number has 14 ones and 3 tens. What is the number?*

**Response:** 3 tens plus another ten from the 14 is 4 tens, plus the 4 ones is 44.

---

**Task:** *85 = 7 tens and _____ ones.*

**Response:** 85 is 8 tens and 5 ones. 8 tens take away 7 tens gives 1 ten. And 1 ten and 5 ones is the same as 15 ones.

---

**Task:** *(7 tens and 16 ones) – (5 tens and 9 ones) =*

**Response:** 7 tens minus 5 tens is 2 tens; 16 ones minus 9 ones is 7 ones; 2 tens and 7 ones is 27.

---

**Task:** $3 \times 40 =$

**Response:** 3 times 4 tens is 12 tens, which is 120.

**Task:** *Find 160 divided by 20.*

**Response:** This is like finding how many sets of 2 ten-blocks can be made from 16 ten-blocks. 16 tens divided by 2 tens equals 8.

*For strategies to help students at Level 3.2, see Chapter 3, page 59.*

## Level 3.3  Student integrates levels 2.1, 2.2, 3.1, and 3.2.

Students integrate Levels 2.1, 2.2, 3.1, and 3.2, and they can easily shift among them. For ones, tens, and hundreds, students understand the relation between adjacent place values (moving from one digit to the next digit to the *left, multiplies* the digit's value by ten; moving from one digit to the next digit to the *right, divides* the digit's value by ten). This level is more global than the others and requires observations of a student's work on several tasks to evaluate. Occasionally, however, a student will give some evidence for being at Level 3.3 on a single task, especially if asked sufficient questions.

### EXAMPLES

**Task:** *There are 27 squares under the mat. How many squares are there altogether?*

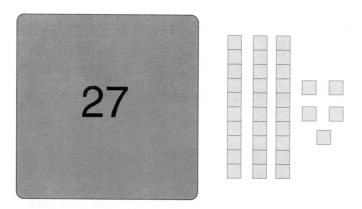

**Response:** 3 tens plus 2 more tens from the 27 is 5 tens or 50; 7 plus 5 is 12. 62. *[Teacher: How do you know you're correct?]* 10, 20, 30, 40, 50 plus 12 is 62.

In her first response, the student uses tens language (Level 3.2). In her second response she uses counting by tens (Level 2.1).

**Task:** *(7 tens and 16 ones) – (5 tens and 9 ones) =*

**Response:** 7 tens take away 5 tens is 2 tens; 16 ones minus 9 ones is 7 ones; 2 tens and 7 ones is 27. *[Teacher: Why is that true?]* Well, there's 70 minus 50 *[pointing to the 7 tens then the 5 tens]*; that's 20. Then 16 minus 9 equals 7. So it's 27.

In his first response, the student uses tens language (Level 3.2). In his second response, he uses multiples of tens language (Level 3.1).

---

**Task:** *A number has 23 tens and 6 ones. What is the number?*

**Response:** Twenty tens is 2 hundreds and 3 tens. So that's two hundred plus thirty, which is 230. And 6 ones; that's 236.

This student uses a mixture of tens language and multiples-of-tens language.

---

**Task:** $5 \times (3 \text{ tens}) =$
$5 \times 30 =$

**Response:** Five times 3 tens is 15 tens. 10 tens is a hundred. So 15 tens is 1 hundred and 5 tens, which is 150. Five times 30 is 150 because you have 5 groups of 30. You get the same answer because 3 tens equals thirty.

This student used tens/hundreds language on the first part of the problem and multiples-of-ten language on the second part.

*For strategies to help students at Level 3.3, see Chapter 3, page 60.*

## LEVEL 4: Student Understands Place Value in Expanded Algorithms

An algorithm is a fixed sequence of steps that solves one type of problem. At Level 4, students understand and meaningfully use expanded paper-and-pencil algorithms for arithmetic operations. In an expanded algorithm, numbers are treated in their place-value "expanded" form (for example, 35 is treated as "thirty plus five"), and the results of intermediate operations are shown in their entirety. The place-value parts of the numbers are retained both in words and symbols. (In the traditional algorithm, place value is dealt with implicitly by the position of the digits, not in the language—so place values are hidden.)

Students who are reasoning at Level 3 have the conceptual understanding necessary to understand expanded algorithms. However, that understanding does not automatically occur. Students must explicitly use their place-value understanding to make sense of expanded algorithms—which happens at Level 4.

Expanded algorithms are extremely important for two reasons. First, expanded algorithms provide students a way to organize and make efficient the concept-rich reasoning they develop in Level 3. Fluent use of such algorithms reduces the cognitive load on students as they perform computations, making it less likely that they will produce errors because they get lost in performing complex procedures. Second, expanded algorithms provide students with the conceptual knowledge they need to understand traditional adult algorithms.

## Level 4.1 Student understands place value in expanded addition and subtraction algorithms.

Students' understanding of place value is sufficient for them to understand and use expanded algorithms for addition and subtraction. They are proficient with decomposing numbers into their place-value parts, then operating on those parts in ways that are consistent with place-value concepts and properties of numbers. Note that when using some expanded algorithms, students do not have to deal with ones first, then tens, then hundreds, as with traditional algorithms. They can, and often do, operate on hundreds first, then tens, then ones.

### EXAMPLES

**Task:** *342 + 435 =*

**Response 1:** Three hundred forty-two is three hundred plus forty plus two; four hundred thirty-five is four hundred plus thirty plus five. Three hundred plus four hundred equals seven hundred; forty plus thirty equals seventy; two plus five is seven. So it's seven hundred seventy-seven.

$$300 + 40 + 2$$
$$+ 400 + 30 + 5$$
$$700 + 70 + 7 = 777$$

**Response 2:** Three hundred plus four hundred equals seven hundred; forty plus thirty equals seventy; two plus five is seven. So it's seven hundred seventy-seven.

$$342$$
$$+ 435$$
$$700$$
$$70$$
$$7$$
$$777$$

The key difference between Responses 1 and 2 is that Response 1 rewrites each addend decomposed into its place-value parts, whereas Response 2 treats the numbers as being decomposed into their place value parts but does not write these parts separately. Response 2 is a bit closer in format to the traditional algorithm.

**Task:** *535 – 342 =*

**Response 1:** 5 – 2 = 3. You can't take 40 from 30, so I have to take 100 from the 500 and add it to the 30. *[Rewriting the problem as shown below]* That makes the 30 into 130 and the 500 into 400. So, 130 – 40 = 90; 400 – 300 = 100. 100 + 90 + 3 = 193.

| | Rewriting |
|---|---|
| 500 + 30 + 5 ——> <br> – (300 + 40 + 2) <br> 3 | 400 + 130 + 5 <br> – (300 +   40 + 2) <br> 100 +   90 + 3 = 193 |

**Response 2:** *[Writing as shown below]* Five hundred minus three hundred equals two hundred. Thirty minus forty equals minus ten.  Five minus two equals three. Two hundred minus ten is one hundred ninety, plus three, equals one hundred ninety three.

$$
\begin{array}{r}
535 \\
-\ 342 \\
\hline
200 \quad 500 - 300 = 200 \\
-10 \quad 30 - 40 = -10 \\
\underline{\phantom{00}3} \quad 5 - 2 = 3 \\
193
\end{array}
$$

*For strategies to help students at Level 4.1, see Chapter 3, pages 65 and 66.*

## Level 4.2  Student understands place value in expanded multiplication and division algorithms.

Students' understanding of place value is sufficient for them to understand and use expanded algorithms for multiplication and division. They are proficient with decomposing numbers into their place-value parts, then operating on those parts in ways that are consistent with place-value concepts and properties of numbers, especially the distributive property.

To implement Level 4.2 reasoning with proficiency, students need to be able to multiply multiples of 10 mentally. That is, they should be fairly fluent with mentally computing problems such as 20 times 60.

**Task:** *45 × 34 =*

**Response:** 40 times 30 is—4 times 3 is 12 add the two zeros—one-thousand two-hundred. 30 times 5 is 150 because 3 times 5 is 15 and add the zero, 150. 40 times 4 is 160 because 4 times 4 is 16 and just add the zero. 4 times 5 is 20. Add 1200, 150, 160, and 20 and you get 1,540. *[Student made an addition error.]*

$$30 \times 40 = 1200$$
$$30 \times 5 = 150$$
$$40 \times 4 = 160$$
$$4 \times 5 = 20$$
$$\overline{1,540}$$

**Task:** *Mary has 84 cookies. She wants to divide them equally among four people. How many cookies does each person get?*

**Response:** I think you are going to have to divide 84 by 4. Four times 3 is 12 *[recording 3 in the right of the problem].* 72 *[subtracting 12 from 84].* 10 groups *[recording 10 under the 3].* 40. 32 *[subtracting 40 from 72].* 4 times 5 is 20. 12 *[subtracting 20 from 32].* And 3 times 4 is 12 again. 12 and 12 cancel each other out; zero, zero. So you would add these together: 10 plus 5 is 15, plus 3 is 18, then another 3 is 21. So each person would get 21 cookies.

$$4\overline{)84}$$

**Task:** *490 divided by 14.*

**Response:** I would do the alternate algorithm way. *[Subtracts 140 from the 490, getting 350, and writes 10 × 14 to the side of her work. Subtracts another 140 and now has 210. Subtracts another 10 × 14, or 140, from the 210 and gets 130. Checks her subtraction and changes the 130 to 70. Subtracts 5 × 14, or 70, from the 70. Adds the partial quotients she had written on the right side by counting by tens.]* 10, 20, 30, 35 *[points to each multiplication].* 35.

$$14\overline{)490}$$
$$-\,140 \rightarrow 10 \times 14$$
$$\overline{\phantom{-}350}$$
$$-\,140 \rightarrow 10 \times 14$$
$$\overline{\phantom{-}210}$$
$$-\,140 \rightarrow 10 \times 14$$
$$\overline{\phantom{-}70}$$
$$-\;\,70 \rightarrow 5 \times 14$$
$$\overline{\phantom{-}0}$$

## More Examples of Students' Use of Expanded Multiplication Algorithms

| $53 \times 4 = ?$ | $53 \times 24 = ?$ | $53 \times 24 = ?$ |
|---|---|---|
| 53<br>$\times 4$<br>———<br>12<br>200<br>———<br>212 | 53<br>$\times 24$<br>———<br>12 $\quad 4 \times 3$<br>200 $\quad 4 \times 50$<br>60 $\quad 20 \times 3$<br>1000 $\quad 20 \times 50$<br>———<br>1272 | $(50 + 3)$<br>$\times (20 + 4)$<br>————————<br>$4 \times \;\;3 \quad\quad 12$<br>$4 \times 50 \quad\quad 200$<br>$20 \times \;\;3 \quad\quad 60$<br>$20 \times 50 \quad\quad 1000$<br>————————<br>1272 |
| **Response:** *4 times 3 is 12; write 12.*<br><br>*4 times 50 is 200; write 200.*<br><br>*200 plus 12 is 212.* | **Response:** *4 times 3 is 12; write 12.*<br><br>*4 times 50 is 200; write 200.*<br><br>*20 times 3 is 60; write 60.*<br><br>*20 times 50 is 1000; write 1000.*<br><br>*12 plus 200 equals 212,*<br><br>*plus 60 equals 272,*<br><br>*plus 1000 equals 1272.* | **Response:** *53 equals 50 + 3.*<br>*24 equals 20 + 4.*<br><br>*4 times 3 is 12; write 12.*<br><br>*4 times 50 is 200; write 200.*<br><br>*20 times 3 is 60; write 60.*<br><br>*20 times 50 is 1000; write 1000.*<br><br>*Now add them up.*<br><br>*2 + 0 + 0 + 0 = 0.*<br><br>*10 + 60 = 70, write the 7.*<br><br>*200 write the 2.*<br><br>*Plus 1000, write the 1.*<br><br>*So it's 1272.* |

| More Examples of Students' Use of Expanded Division Algorithms | |
|---|---|
| 528 ÷ 7 = ? (solution 1)<br><br>528 ÷ 7 = ?<br><br>$7\overline{)528}$<br>　$-350$　(50 × 7)<br>　178<br>　$-140$　(20 × 7)<br>　　38<br>　　$-35$　　(5 × 7)<br>　　　3　　　75<br><br>Answer: 75 r3 | 528 ÷ 7 = ? (solution 2)<br><br>$7\overline{)528}$<br>　$-490$　70<br>　　38<br>　　$-35$　　5<br>　　　3　75<br><br>Answer: 75 r3 |
| **Less efficient** | **More efficient** |
| *How many times can I subtract 7 from 528? (How many 7s are in 528?)*<br><br>*Can I subtract 100 sevens? No.*<br><br>*If I subtract fifty 7s, I am subtracting 350, with 178 left over.*<br><br>*If I subtract twenty 7s from 178, I have 38 left over.*<br><br>*If I subtract five 7s from 38, I have 3 left over.*<br><br>*So I have subtracted a total of 50 + 20 + 5 = 75 sevens, and I have 3 left over as a remainder.* | *How many times can I subtract 7 from 528?*<br><br>*Can I subtract 100 sevens? No.*<br><br>*Can I subtract 70 sevens? Yes.*<br><br>*Can I subtract 80 sevens? No.*<br><br>*So subtract 70 sevens, that is, 490, with 38 left over.*<br><br>*Subtract 5 sevens, and get 3 left.*<br><br>*So I have subtracted a total of 70 + 5 = 75 sevens, and I have 3 left over as a remainder.* |

*For strategies to help students at Level 4.2, see Chapter 3, pages 65–69.*

## LEVEL 5: Student Understands Place Value in Traditional Algorithms

Students use their understanding of place value and other properties of numbers to conceptually understand traditional algorithms for whole-number arithmetic, even though place value ideas in these algorithms are hidden. In addition to understanding numbers as combinations of their place-value parts, students understand and can move flexibly between various place-value parts. For example, students understand that the 2 in 243 can be thought of as 200 ones, 2 hundreds, or 20 tens. This understanding enables them to understand the regrouping processes ("carrying" and "borrowing") performed in the algorithms.

The key idea in Level 5 is determining whether students conceptually understand traditional algorithms. They can demonstrate this understanding by using language that shows they are decomposing numbers into their place-value parts. They also can demonstrate understanding by explicitly showing how traditional algorithms correspond step-by-step to expanded algorithms.

## Level 5.1  Student understands place value in traditional addition and subtraction algorithms.

Students *understand* and use traditional addition and subtraction algorithms.

### EXAMPLES

**Task:**

$$\begin{array}{r} 63 \\ -38 \\ \hline \end{array}$$

**Response:** 3 – 8, you can't do that, it'd be negative. So I'm gonna make this a 50 and put the ten into the 3, so that's a 13. Now 13 – 8 = 5 *[writes 5 underneath the 8]*. And 50 – 30 = 20 *[writes 2 underneath the 3 in 38]*.

$$\begin{array}{r} \overset{50}{\cancel{6}}\overset{13}{\cancel{3}} \\ -\ 38 \\ \hline 25 \end{array}$$

**Task:** *267 + 189 =*

**Response:** *[Puts 189 under 267 and adds vertically, right to left]* 7 + 9 is 6, put the 1 up *[writes 1 above 6]*. 8 and 6 is 14 add the 1, that's 15. Put the 5 down, put the 1 up, add the 1, 2, and 1; that's 4.

$$\begin{array}{r} \overset{1}{2}\overset{1}{6}7 \\ +\ 189 \\ \hline 456 \end{array}$$

*[Teacher: Why does this method work?]* Because 7 plus 9 equals 16, which is 1 ten and 6 ones—so write 6 and put 1 ten above 6 tens. Then 1 ten plus 6 tens plus 8 tens equals 15 tens. That's 1 hundred—I put 1 above the 2 hundreds—and 5 tens in the tens place. 1 hundred plus 2 hundreds plus 1 hundred is 4 hundred, so put 4 in the hundreds place. I got 456.

Although this student performed the traditional algorithm using language that did not indicate the place values of numbers, when his teacher asked him why the method worked, his answer clearly indicated that he understood the place-value concepts that justified each step in the algorithm.

**Task:** *46 – 17 =*

**Response:** Take 1 ten from the 4 tens and add it to the 6 to make 16. 16 minus 7 equals 9. 3 tens minus 1 ten equals 2 tens.

$$\begin{array}{r} \overset{3\ \ 16}{4\cancel{6}} \\ -17 \\ \hline 29 \end{array}$$

**Task:** *46 + 17 =*

**Response:** 6 plus 7 equals 13. Put down the 3 and bring 1 ten over to the tens column. 1 ten plus 4 tens plus 1 ten equals 6 tens, write 6 in the tens column.

$$\begin{array}{r} \overset{1}{4}6 \\ +17 \\ \hline 63 \end{array}$$

The language the student used in the two problems above suggests that she understands the place-value basis for the traditional algorithms.

*For strategies to help students at Level 5.1, see Chapter 3, page 70.*

## Level 5.2 Student understands place value in traditional multiplication and division algorithms.

At this level, students *understand* and use traditional multiplication and division algorithms. Because the traditional multiplication and division algorithms are more complicated than the traditional addition and subtraction algorithms, even students who understand them will generally not use language that makes place value evident. To determine if these students understand the place-value aspects of these algorithms, we generally have to ask appropriate questions, as illustrated below. (Another way that students can demonstrate understanding of the traditional algorithm is to show how it's related to an expanded algorithm. See *Cognition-Based Assessment: Multiplication and Division*.)

**Task:** *45 × 23 =*

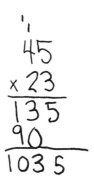

**Response:** *[As he writes]* 3 times 5 is 15, write the 5, put the ten up here in the tens column *[writes 1 above 4]*. 3 times 4 is 12, plus 1 is 13 *[writes 13]*. 2 times 5 is 10, write the 0, put the 1 above the 4 *[writing 0 below the 3 in the first partial product and the 1 above ]*. 2 times 4 is 8 plus 1 is 9.

> **Teacher:** Why did you write the 13 to the left of 5, why didn't you just add 13 to 5 *[pointing]*?
>
> **Student:** Because the 13 is really 130, so the 13 has to go in the tens and hundreds places.
>
> **Teacher:** Why is the 13 really 130?
>
> **Student:** Because you're multiplying 3 times 40; the 4 here stands for 40.
>
> **Teacher:** Why did you write the 0 from 2 times 5 here [pointing]?
>
> **Student:** Because it's really 20 times 5, which is 100. That's why I put the little 1 over here, in hundreds.
>
> **Teacher:** Where does the 90 come from?
>
> **Student:** It's really 900. It's 20 times 45.

*For strategies to help students at Level 5.2, see Chapter 3, page 70.*

## LEVEL 6: Student Generalizes Place-Value Understanding to Large Numbers, Numbers Less Than 1, and Exponential Notation

At Level 6, students extend their understanding of place value beyond hundreds to thousands, ten-thousands, hundred-thousands, millions, and so on, depending on grade level. They can properly name large numbers, taking into account their "periods." As can be seen in the whole numbers place-value chart, moving right to left, the periods are: ones, thousands, millions, billions, trillions, and so on. To say a number, say the number of hundreds, tens, and ones in the standard way, followed by the period name, going left to right. So, for example, we say the number 465,843,579: Four-hundred sixty-five million, eight-hundred forty-three thousand, five-hundred seventy-nine.

Students' understanding of place value for larger numbers also involves knowing the place values of digits in larger numbers. In the whole numbers example, 6 has the value six ten-millions; 8 has the value eight hundred-thousands. Another component of understanding place value of larger numbers is being able to construct a number, given its place-value parts. For instance, students can write and say the number described by the sum 9 ten-thousands + 8 hundreds + 3 ones.

Students also extend their understanding of place value to positive numbers less than 1 (see chart at right), which involves a different naming scheme than for numbers larger than 1. Students understand, for instance, how to name decimal numbers that include decimal fractions and understand the place value for each place. For example, students know to say the number .4325 as "four-thousand three-hundred twenty-five *ten-thousandths*." So in naming a decimal less than 1, the last digit to the right determines the decimal fraction value given to the number (ten-thousandths for .4325). Students also understand that in .4325, the value of 4 is 4 tenths, the value of 3 is 3 hundredths, the value of 2 is 2 thousandths, and the value of 5 is 5 ten-thousandths. Finally, students understand that four-thousand three-hundred twenty-five ten-thousandths = 4 tenths + 3 hundredths + 2 thousandths + 5 ten-thousandths (.4325 = .4 + .03 + .002 + .0005).

Students also extend their understanding of place value to recognize the exponential structure of the base-ten place-value system. Place values can be expressed in terms of powers of 10 using exponents. For instance, $10^3$ means 10 multiplied together 3 times—10 times 10 times 10. In this case, 3 is the exponent. Negative exponents indicate that the power of 10 occurs in the denominator of the fraction.

Finally, at Level 6, students understand the relationship between adjacent place values, for all numbers, large and small. That is, moving from one digit to the next digit to the left multiplies the digit's value by 10 (so adds 1 to the exponent of 10), whereas moving from one digit to the next digit to the right divides the digit's value by 10 (so subtracts 1 from the exponent of 10).

## Place-Value Chart for Whole Numbers

| Periods | MILLIONS | | | THOUSANDS | | | ONES | | |
|---|---|---|---|---|---|---|---|---|---|
| Value within Period | hundreds | tens | ones | hundreds | tens | ones | hundreds | tens | ones |
| Place Value | hundred millions | ten millions | one millions | hundred thousands | ten thousands | one thousands | hundreds | tens | ones |
| Place-Value Number | 100,000,000 | 10,000,000 | 1,000,000 | 100,000 | 10,000 | 1,000 | 100 | 10 | 1 |
| Example | 4 | 6 | 5 | 8 | 4 | 3 | 5 | 7 | 9 |

## Place-Value Chart for Numbers Less Than 1

| Place Value | ones | tenths | hundredths | thousandths | ten-thousandths | hundred-thousandths | millionths |
|---|---|---|---|---|---|---|---|
| Place-Value Number | 1 | .1 = 1/10 | .01 = 1/100 | .001 = 1/1000 | .0001 = 1/10000 | .00001 = 1/100000 | .000001 = 1/1000000 |
| Example | . | 4 | 3 | 2 | 5 | 5 | |

## Saying Larger Numbers

**Task:** *Say or write this number: 843,567.*

**Response:** Eight-hundred forty-three thousand, five hundred sixty-seven.

## Recognizing and Adding/Subtracting Larger Numbers, Given Their Place-Value Parts

**Task:** *9 ten-thousands + 8 hundreds + 3 =*

**Response 1:** Write a 9 for ten-thousand; there are no thousands, so put 0; write 8 for hundreds; no tens, so put 0; write 3. *[Writes 90803] [Teacher: How do you say this number?]* Nine ten-thousands, eight hundred three. No, wait. Ninety-thousand, eight hundred three.

**Response 2:** I used the Place-Value Chart. I put a 9 in the ten-thousands column, an 8 in the hundreds column, and a 3 in the ones column. Then I put zeros in the in-between columns. I got the number 90803.

**Task:** *3 thousands – 8 hundreds =*

**Response 1:** One thousand equals 10 hundreds. Take away 8 hundreds and you have 2 hundreds left. Add that to the other 2 thousands. So 2 thousand 2 hundred is the answer.

**Response 2:** I used the Place-Value Chart. I put 3 in the thousands column and got 3000. Below that, I put 8 in the hundreds column and got 800. I subtracted and got 2200.

In this task, Response 1 is more sophisticated than Response 2 because it explicitly shows understanding of the relationship between adjacent place values (1 thousand equals 10 hundreds).

## Decimal Numbers Less Than 1

**Task:** *Explain why 53 hundredths (.53) equals 5 tenths (.5) plus 3 hundredths (.03).*

**Response:** Use fractions.

$$5 \text{ tenths} + 3 \text{ hundredths} = \frac{5}{10} + \frac{3}{100} = \frac{50}{100} + \frac{3}{100} = \frac{53}{100} = 53 \text{ hundredths}$$

So students' understanding of fractions contributes to their understanding of decimals. (See *Cognition-Based Assessment and Teaching of Fractions* for more on students' understanding of fractions.)

## Exponential Notation for Expanded Form

**Task:** *Express 5634.792 in expanded form in at least two ways.*

**Response 1:** 5000 + 600 + 30 + 4 + 7/10 + 9/100 + 2/1000

**Response 2:** $5634.792 = 5 \times (1000) + 6 \times (100) + 3 \times (10) + 4 + 7 \times (1/10) + 9 \times (1/100) + 2 \times (1/1000)$

**Response 3:** $5634.792 = 5 \times (10^3) + 6 \times (10^2) + 3 \times (10^1) + 4 \times (10^0) + 7 \times (10^{-1}) + 9 \times (10^{-2}) + 2 \times (10^{-3})$

# Using CBA Levels to Develop a Profile of a Student's Reasoning About Place Value

CBA assessment tasks are designed to help you assess levels of reasoning, not levels of students. Indeed, a student might use different levels of reasoning on different tasks. For instance, a student might operate at a higher level when using physical materials such as base-ten blocks than when she does not have physical materials to support her thinking. Also, a student might operate at different levels on tasks that are familiar to her, or that she has practiced, as opposed to tasks that are totally new to her. So, rather than attempting to assign a single level to a student, you should analyze a student's reasoning on several assessment tasks, then develop an overall profile of how she is reasoning about the topic.

To develop a CBA profile of a student's reasoning, note which CBA assessment tasks you give to the student, the date, and what CBA level of reasoning the student used on each task. Note whether the student used concrete materials (CM), drew pictures (D), used paper-and-pencil to write computations (PP), or did the problem strictly mentally (M). Record whether the student answered the questions correctly or not (C or I). Some teachers also note whether a student was being guided by a teacher (T) or worked on the task without any help (WH). These annotations can be quite important in monitoring student progress. For instance, if in the initial assessment a student uses one level of reasoning with the help of concrete materials but in a subsequent assessment the student uses the same level of reasoning implemented mentally, the student has made considerable progress.

As shown next, a CBA profile provides an excellent picture of student reasoning that can be monitored throughout the school year.

## DS, Grade 2, Place Value

1. Mary has 24 cookies. She eats 6 of them. How many cookies are left?

   **DS:** *24. 24 subtract 6. 24.* [Now, for each of the following numbers, DS extends a finger as he counts.] *23, 22, 21, 19, 18, 17.*

2. In a box, there are 35 red apples and 27 green apples. How many apples are in the box?

   **DS:** [Grabs 3 ten-blocks]...*10, 20, 30. Then* [grabs 5 one-blocks and places them next to the ten-blocks] *35.* [Grabs 2 ten-blocks then one-blocks, 2 at a time] *20, 22, 24, 26, 27. I've got 27 green apples and 35 red apples.* [Moves the 3 ten-blocks next to the 2 ten-blocks] *And so 30* [pauses for 7 seconds] *50.* [Moves the one-blocks together, but still in groups of 7 and 5] *51, 52, 53, 54, 55, 56, 57, 58, 59, 60, 61, 62.*

3. 47 + 24

   **DS:** *I added 7 and 4...it was 11. So then I put a 1 right here [in solution] and a 1 up here [above 4 in 47] and then I put 1 + 4 + 2 and it equals 7.* [Teacher: Okay, and then you got 71.] *Yeah.* [Teacher: So what does this 1 (above the 4 in 47) stand for?] *To add with the 4 and the 2.* [Teacher: Is it just a 1?] *Yes.*

4. (with blocks). Use the place-value blocks to solve this problem.

   36
   +28

   **DS:** *I've got 36 and 28.* [Picks up the 2 ten-blocks from 28] *20.* [Picks up the 3 ten-blocks from 36 and lays them down] *30.* [Points to one of the 2 ten-blocks from 28 in his hand, then lays down the 2 ten-blocks] *40, 50.* [Places the one-blocks from both piles together and counts them, one at a time.] *51, 52, 53, 54, 55, 56, 57, 58, 59, 60, 61, 62, 63, 64.* [Writes "64" on his paper.] *64.*

   (no blocks). Solve this problem without blocks.

   36
   +28

   **DS:** *6 and 8.* [Counts starting with 9] *9, 10, 11, 12, 13, 14.* [Writes 1 above the 3 in the tens column and 4 in the ones place in the answer space.] *1, 4.* [Counts] *5, 6.* [Writes 6 in the tens place next to the 4 in the ones place] *64.* [Teacher: Okay. And how'd you get that?] *'Cause I did 6 + 8 is*

*14. So then I put the 4 down here and the 1 up top, and then 3 + 2. I mean 1 + 3 + 2 is 6.* [Teacher: So explain to me how these two ways of doing the problem are alike and different.] *I don't know what you're saying.*

Note that students who really understand place value make sense of and can correctly answer this question.

5. Circle how many dots this part *[circles the numeral 2 in 23]* of the number means.

   **DS:** *I think it's this* [circles 2 dots in the group of 3 dots]. [Teacher: Okay. And how do you know that?] *Because these two are 2* [pointing to the 2 dots he circled] *and this is 2* [pointing to the 2 in 23].

6. There are 25 squares under the card. How many squares are there altogether?

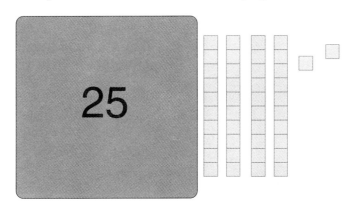

   **DS:** *So, 25 squares under this* [pointing at the card], *and there'd be* [pointing at columns of ten and counting by tens, then counting the last 2 squares individually] *35, 45, 55, 65, 66, 67. 67.*

7. 7 + 600 + 40 = _____

   **DS:** *Well, 4 + 6 is 7, 8, 9* [pause]; *I really don't know this.*

8. 555 − 5 = _____

   **DS:** *55, 54, 53, 52, 51. Wait, messed up. 54, 55, fifty—I keep messing up.* [Teacher: Do you need to keep track on your fingers? Would that help?] *55, 54, 53, 52, 51, 50* [extending a finger for every number from 54 down to 50]. [Teacher: Okay, so what's your answer?] *550.*

**9.**

If I'm at building 17, and I go forward 5 buildings, where am I?

> **DS:** [Counts forward 5 buildings from 17 until he reaches building 22] *1, 2, 3, 4, 5. 22.*

If I'm at building 17, and I go forward 10 buildings, where am I?

> **DS:** [Counts forward 10 buildings from 17 until he reaches building 27] *1, 2, 3, 4, 5, 6, 7, 8, 9, 10 . . . 27.*

If I'm at building 17, and I go forward 20 buildings, where am I?

> **DS:** [Counts forward from 17 until he runs out of buildings at 30] *1, 2, 3, 4, 5, 6, 7, 8, 9, 10, 11, 12, 13. [Pause.] It's no more . . . .*

**10.** 46 = _____ tens and _____ ones.

> **Teacher:** *46* [points at 46] *is how many tens* [points at blank next to "tens"] *and how many ones* [points at blank next to "ones"]?

> **DS:** [Writes 4 next to "tens"] *4 tens and* [writes 6 next to "ones"] *6 ones.*

> **Teacher:** *Good. And how do you know that?*

> **DS:** *Because I learned that 4 goes next to the tens and the 6 goes next to the ones.*

**11.** Jon has 2 packs of gum and 8 sticks of gum. There are 10 sticks in each pack. How many <u>sticks</u> of gum does Jon have altogether?

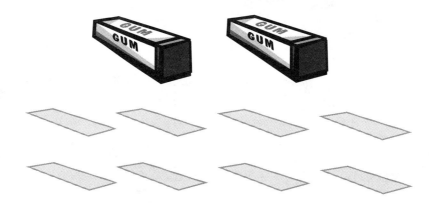

**DS:** [Says immediately] *28.* [Teacher: Okay, how'd you get that?] *Because I had 10 that's in here* [pointing at 2 packs] *and that was 20, and then I added these 8* [pointing to 8 sticks at bottom] *and I got 28.*

12. 85 = 7 tens *and* _____ ones.

> **DS:** [Writes 85.] [Teacher: And how'd you get that?] *'Cause the 85 was alone, so I put it in the ones.* [Teacher: Okay. And then these 7 tens just don't matter?] *No.*

13. To do the problem 57 + 32, Bill said:

5 + 3 = 8

7 + 2 = 9

> **Bill said:** *The answer is 8 + 9 = 17. Is Bill correct?*

> **DS:** *Mmm hmm (yes).* [Teacher: Okay, why?] *Because 8 + 9 is 17.*

14. (7 tens and 16 ones) – (5 tens and 9 ones) = _____.

> **DS:** *7 plus 16* [extends a finger for each number, starting with 17, until he has 7 fingers extended] *17, 18, 19, 20, 21, 22, 23. But then* [pointing at "5 tens and 9 ones" and counting backward] *it's 23, 22, 21, 20, 19, 17, 18, 17, 16, 15, 14, 13, 12, 11, 8, 9. So it's 9.* [Teacher: Okay, how'd you get that?] *Because I added these* [pointing to 7 and 16 in problem statement], *then I subtracted from 5 and 9* [pointing at 5 and 9 in problem statement], *and I got 9.*

## **Step 2:** *Construct a CBA Levels Summary Chart for DS*

| Task | Level | Correct/ Incorrect | Comment | Mode* |
|---|---|---|---|---|
| 1 | 0 | I | Counting back error. | F |
| 2 | 2.1 | C | | PVB |
| 3 | 1.3 | C | Thinks IO is I. | PP |
| 4 blocks | 2.1 | C | | PVB |
| 4 no blocks | 1.3 | C | Cannot relate A blocks/no blocks. | PP |
| 5 | 1.3 | I | | M |
| 6 | 2.2 | C | | P |
| 7 | 1.3 | I | | M |
| 8 | 1.1 | C | Guided by teacher. | F |
| 9a | 1.1 | C | | P |
| 9b | 1.1 | C | | P |
| 9c | 1.1 | I | | P |
| 10 | 1.3 | C | Doesn't understand. | M |
| 11 | 2.1 | C | | P |
| 12 | 1.3 | I | | M |
| 13 | 1.3 | I | | M |
| 14 | 1.3 | I | | M |

*concrete materials (C), place-value blocks (PVB), drew pictures (D) or used given picture (P), used paper-and-pencil to write computations (PP), did the problem strictly mentally (M), or with fingers (F).

As can be seen from the previous chart, when using place value representing concrete or pictorial materials, DS operates at Level 2.1 or Level 2.2. However, when such materials are not available, DS reverts to various types of Level 1 reasoning. So our instructional goal is to encourage and support DS' movement to Level 2 *verbally* (without using place-value materials or pictures). To move DS to Level 2 (operating on numbers by skip-counting place-value parts) verbally (he is already able to do this concretely), we have to instructionally fade visual/concrete materials in a way that supports this transition.

## Recommendations

Start trying to accomplish the goal with place-value blocks because DS has had some success at Level 2 reasoning with them. Then move to different contexts to ensure that his Level 2 reasoning is general.

Have DS do a problem and observe if he uses the type of reasoning targeted by that goal. If he does not, you might demonstrate that type of reasoning for him to see if he makes sense of it. But don't demand that he use it.

**PROBLEM TYPE 1** How many ones in each pile? Write the number under the piles.

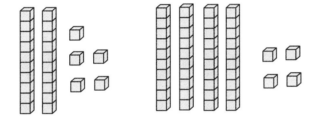

*[Cover the piles, but not the numbers and ask]* How many ones are there altogether under the mats?

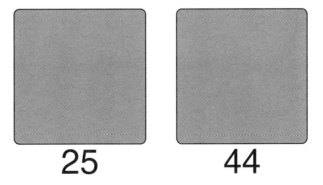

**PROBLEM TYPE 2** Write the problem 25 + 30.

Ask, "How much is 25 plus 30? Can you count by tens? Try to do this problem in your head without writing." If DS cannot do this problem in his head, show him the picture below, and ask the question again.

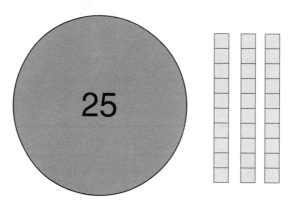

Repeat with additional problems, first adding multiples of ten (like 30, 40, or 20), then later non-multiples of ten (like 33, 46, or 28). Each time, first ask the problem strictly verbally (without a picture). If DS cannot do the problem mentally, ask if counting by tens will help. If DS still cannot do the problem mentally (no algorithm), give a picture.

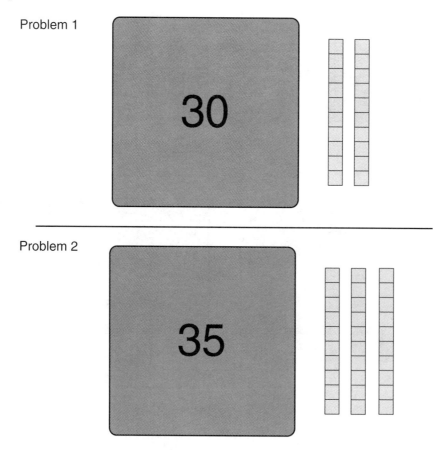

Problem 1

Problem 2

Cognition-Based Assessment and Teaching of Place Value

Problem 3

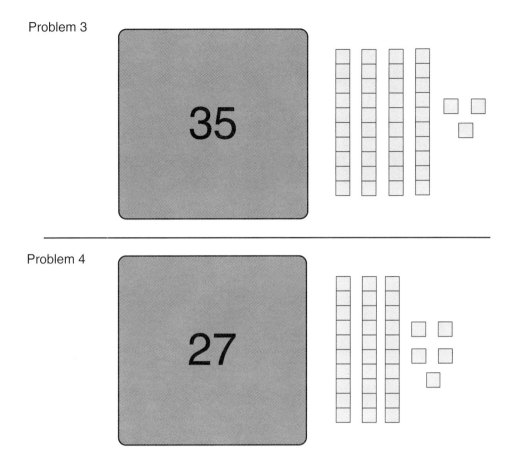

Problem 4

PROBLEM TYPE 3   Have the student do house problems, starting with a multiple of ten and going forward a multiple of ten (just ten at first). We want students to see the linguistic pattern in the counting sequence.

    ▦  If I'm at house 10 and I go forward 10 houses, what house will I be at? Can you figure out the answer without counting by ones? (If not, let DS count by ones.)

    ▦  If I'm at house 20 and I go forward 10 houses, what house will I be at? Can you figure out the answer without counting by ones? (If not, let DS count by ones.)

    ▦  If I'm at house 30 and I go forward 10 houses, what house will I be at? Can you figure out the answer without counting by ones? (If not, let DS count by ones.)

    ▦  If I'm at house 10 and I go forward 10 houses, what house will I be at? Can you figure out the answer without counting by ones? (If not, let DS count by ones.)

- If I'm at house 10 and I go forward 20 houses, what house will I be at? Can you figure out the answer without counting by ones? (If not, let DS count by ones.)

- If I'm at house 10 and I go forward 30 houses, what house will I be at? Can you figure out the answer without counting by ones? (If not, let DS count by ones.)

**PROBLEM TYPE 4 (TRADING)**  Use the place-value blocks to show 34. Is there another way to do this? Encourage DS to see these different ways:

- 3 ten-blocks, 4 one-blocks
- 2 ten-blocks, 14 one-blocks
- 1 ten-block, 24 one-blocks
- 0 ten-blocks, 34 one-blocks

# Chapter 3

## Instructional Strategies for Place Value

Once you have used the CBA assessment tasks to determine which CBA levels of reasoning students are using, you can use the teaching suggestions and instructional tasks described in this chapter to tailor instruction to precisely fit students' learning needs. For each major level of reasoning, there are suggestions for teaching that encourage and support students' movement to the next important type of reasoning in the sequence.

For students to make progress, have them do several problems of a specific type until you see them move to the next level, or you become convinced that they are not quite ready to move on to the next level. In the latter case, try a different kind of problem suggested for that level.

Note that attaining higher levels of reasoning about place value, especially the highest levels, is interrelated with attaining higher levels of reasoning about the arithmetic operations of addition, subtraction, multiplication, and division.

## Teaching Students at Level 0: Constructing Initial Meaning for Object Counting and Numbers

Help students learn the *verbal* count-by-ones sequence. Many young students do not know the verbal sequence ("one, two, three" and so on, or the numerals that correspond to these numbers). Students have particular difficulty learning the names of numbers in the teens, and at transitions between multiples of ten (e.g., from 29 to 30 to 31), and at transitions between hundreds (e.g., from 99 to 100, or from 199 to 200). Even though there is a logical pattern to the sequence of verbal counting words (other than in the teens), it can be difficult initially for young students to make sense of this sequence. One way you can help students learn the verbal sequence is by doing class counts: "Let's all count from 1 to 20." But be sure to monitor students' counts so you know which students can do this on their own. Another way to do this is to do class counts while you point to sets of objects displayed on an overhead projector.

For students who know the verbal sequence but are not reliable in counting sets of objects, start with smaller numbers, then move to larger numbers. Students must learn to organize their counting so that each object in a set is counted once and only once. Various tasks can be used to help students with this organization. At first, students should touch each object as they say a count word for it. But even touching might not be enough. For instance, if you give students a set of 8 checkers and ask how many there are, some students who touch each checker will lose track of which checkers they have touched. You can help these students by having them move counted checkers to another spot on the table. You can also ask students to place each checker in a small plastic sandwich bag one at a time, as they count. Or you can make a ten-frame from a dozen-egg carton and have students count as they put table tennis balls in the 10 indentations. This activity helps students visualize the accumulating number of balls for successive numbers in the count.

You can use other activities with bags to further develop students' understanding of counting. For instance, have students watch as you put 5 marbles in a plastic bag, counting one by one as you go. Ask, "How many marbles are in the bag?" Place another marble in the bag and ask, "How many marbles are in the bag now?" This activity helps students further understand the critical one-more-than relationship for numbers and counting.

Another way to help students keep track of their counting is to ask them to write numerals on pictures of objects. For instance, ask students how many circles and how many squares are shown on **STUDENT SHEET 1** . (All of the student sheets referenced in this chapter can be found at www.heinemann.com/products/E04343 .aspx. (Click on the "Companion Resources" tab.)) Have them show you how they count by writing their count numbers inside the circles and squares. Some students will be able to count correctly but still may have difficulty writing the numerals. You will have to watch these students count to assess their understanding. You can help these students by modeling counting, for example, by putting the correct numerals on the squares on Student Sheet 1 as you count.

Once students can reliably count sets of objects, give them problems to help them understand the relationship between counting and the numerosity (cardinality) of sets: "When we count a set of objects, the last number recited tells how many objects are in the set." For instance, you might place 8 paper plates randomly on one table, then a stack of 10 or more napkins on another table. Ask students, "Can you figure out how to put a napkin on each plate without taking the stack of napkins over to the table with plates on it?" Note that students must understand that counting the number of plates tells you how many napkins they must count so that a one-to-one correspondence between plates and napkins is established. Students who do not understand this relationship would need to take the napkins over to the plate table and distribute one napkin per plate—they would solve the problem by modeling, not counting.

Cognition-Based Assessment and Teaching of Place Value

## Teaching Students at Level 1: Learning to Count Groups of Ten and Skip-Count by Ten

Only two of the sublevels of Level 1 are legitimate as instructional goals—Level 1.1 (counting single objects) and Level 1.2 (counting groups of ten). Level 1.3 reasoning is conceptually insufficient, so it should not be promoted by instruction. However, even though we do not explicitly teach the reasoning in Level 1.3, some students will inevitably still reason in this way.

### Teaching Students at Level 1.1: Moving to Counting Groups of Ten

Use physical materials such as unifix or multilink cubes to pose problems in which students count *groups of ten*. Don't use place-value blocks yet—it's important for students to create the groups of ten. Tasks such as the following will help build students' ability to count groups of ten. Start with problems such as Problem 1, using multiples of ten, and then move to numbers in the mid-decades (like Problem 2).

1. Give the student 30 cubes. Ask, "How many stacks of ten cubes can I make with these cubes?"

2. Give the student 46 cubes. Ask, "How many stacks of ten cubes can I make with 46 cubes?"

### Teaching Students at Level 1.2 or Level 1.3: Moving to Skip-Counting by Tens

To progress from counting by ones to counting by tens, students must come to see the counting-by-tens words—*ten, twenty, thirty*—as signifying the number of ones in successive multiples of ten. So, for example, students must understand that counting two groups of ten objects by tens, "10, 20," gives the same result as counting the same objects by ones, "1, 2, 3, . . . , 19, 20." This is true because the last number students say when they count the objects in the first group of ten by ones is "10," and the last number they say when they continue to count the second group of ten by ones is "20."

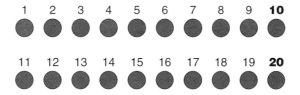

In the problems described below, the goal is for students to determine answers by counting by tens. While doing such problems, many students will notice a pattern that enables them to directly translate between number of tens and number of ones. For instance, these students will see that 4 tens is forty, 6 tens is sixty, and so on. We want students to see this pattern. But we want them to understand why the pattern occurs.

For instance, if a student says that 4 tens is forty, ask, *How do you know?* At this point, we would like the student to justify this answer by counting by tens: "4 tens is forty because if you count to 40 by tens, 10, 20, 30, 40 *[putting up 4 fingers]*, you use 4 tens."

One way to build understanding of skip-counting by ten is to use ten-strips. Show students the 4 ten-strips on an overhead projector or document camera and say, "There are 4 strips of ten squares here. How many squares are there altogether? Can you count by tens?" If students cannot count by tens, have them count the squares by ones, writing the numbers as shown below. After students count by ones, point to the 10, 20, 30, and 40 at the bottoms of the strips and say, "When we counted the squares by ones, look at the last number I said for each strip—10, 20, 30, and 40. Is there a faster way to count them? If no student suggests counting by tens, ask, "What if I count like this: *ten, twenty, thirty, forty*? Why do I still get 40?"

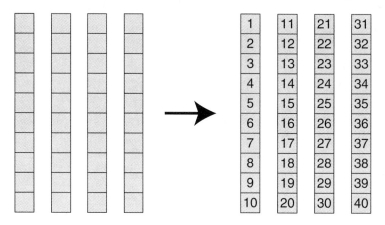

Ask students how many squares there will be if there are 3 strips of ten; 5 strips of ten; "Can you count by tens?" To reinforce the connection between counting by ones and counting by tens, have students check their answers to problems such as 5 strips of ten; have the whole class count the squares by ones with you. (Because the numbers are large, if students count squares individually, they will often make counting mistakes even if they understand counting fairly well.)

Another strategy is to use place-value blocks (or pictures of the blocks). Show 1 ten-block and ask, "How many one-blocks are there in this ten-block? How do you know?" Then show 2 ten-blocks, 3 ten-blocks, and so on, each time asking how many one-blocks there are. If a student finds an answer by counting by ones, ask if there is another, faster way to count.

You can also use a hundred chart as shown on **STUDENT SHEET 2** . For example *[point to 30 on the chart]*, "How many squares are there in the first three rows of the hundreds chart? How did you count? Is there a faster way to count?" Repeat for other decade numbers like 50 and 70. For students who do not see this "faster way to count," return to the initial activities in this section.

You can also give students place-value house problems, starting with a multiple of ten and going forward by a multiple of ten (just ten at first). We want students to see the numeric pattern in the counting sequence.

You can use sets of questions such as the following to help students see the patterns.

## Pattern 1

- If I'm at house 10 and I go forward 10 houses, what house will I be at? Can you figure out the answer without counting by ones? (If not, let students count by ones.)
- If I'm at house 20 and I go forward 10 houses, what house will I be at? Can you figure out the answer without counting by ones? (If not, let students count by ones.)
- If I'm at house 30 and I go forward 10 houses, what house will I be at? Can you figure out the answer without counting by ones? (If not, let students count by ones.)

If students have difficulty seeing Pattern 1, ask questions that relate this pattern to the analogous pattern in counting by ones. After students see the pattern below, return to the house questions above.

- What number is 1 more than 1? What number is 10 more than 10?
- What number is 1 more than 2? What number is 10 more than 20?
- What number is 1 more than 3? What number is 10 more than 30?

## Pattern 2

- If I'm at house 10 and I go forward 10 houses, what house will I be at? Can you figure out the answer without counting by ones? (If not, ask if counting by tens would help. If that does not help, let the student count by ones.)
- If I'm at house 10 and I go forward 20 houses, what house will I be at? Can you figure out the answer without counting by ones? (If not, ask if counting by tens would help. If that does not help, let the student count by ones.)
- If I'm at house 10 and I go forward 30 houses, what house will I be at? Can you figure out the answer without counting by ones? (If not, ask if counting by tens would help. If that does not help, let the student count by ones.)
- If I'm at house 20 and I go forward 30 houses, what house will I be at? Can you figure out the answer without counting by ones? (If not, ask if counting by tens would help. If that does not help, let the student count by ones.)

If students have difficulty seeing Pattern 2, ask questions that relate this pattern to the analogous pattern in counting by ones. After students see the pattern below, return to the house questions above.

- What number is 1 more than 1? What number is 10 more than 10?
- What number is 2 more than 1? What number is 20 more than 10?

▦ What number is 3 more than 1? What number is 30 more than 10?

▦ What number is 3 more than 2? What number is 30 more than 20?

Another way to help students with Pattern 2 is to help them see that finding the number that is 3 more than 1 can be accomplished by finding the number that is 1 more than 1, then 1 more than 2, then 1 more than 3. Similarly, finding the number that is 30 more than 10 can be accomplished by finding the number that is 10 more than 10, then 10 more than 20, then 10 more than 30.

Problems such as those below help give students a real-world context for counting by ten.

*Jon has 3 packs of gum. There are 10 sticks in each pack. How many sticks of gum does Jon have altogether?*

*Jon has 8 sticks of gum and 6 packs of gum. There are 10 sticks in each pack. How many sticks of gum does Jon have altogether?*

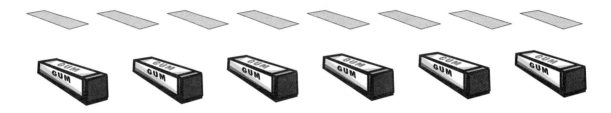

## Teaching Students at Level 2: Extending Understanding of Skip-Counting by Ten

### Teaching Students at Level 2.1: Moving to Counting by Tens and Ones in Mid-Decades

Students must extend their knowledge of counting patterns from counting by tens and ones separately to counting by tens and ones in mid-decades.

Have students do several hidden strips tasks such as those on **STUDENT SHEET 3** ⬇, in which a multiple of ten is added to a two-digit number that is not a multiple of ten, like 37 + 20. We want students to see the numeric pattern in the counting sequence (e.g., to find ten more than 37, increase the tens digit by one to get 47). Once students understand this pattern, present problems in which students add 2 two-digit numbers that are not multiples of ten (such as those on **STUDENT SHEET 4** ⬇ ). Problems in which adding the ones does not cross decades (or require regrouping) will be easier for some students. For example, 23 + 45 will be easier than 28 + 45. For students having difficulty seeing these patterns, you can return to work on the hundred chart and the place value house picture, contexts that add visual support to seeing the patterns.

Give problems in which students must increase or decrease various numbers by multiples of ten on the hundred chart. For instance, point to 7 on the chart. Ask, "If I count forward 10 squares from 7, where will I land?" After getting some answers, demonstrate by pointing to squares: "8, 9, 10, 11, 12, 13, 14, 15, 16, 17. So we land on 17. If I go forward another ten, where do I land? Another?" You can then help students generalize by asking questions such as, "If I start at 7 and count by tens, what numbers do I land on? How do you know?"

Students should also attend to how many tens they count by. For instance, ask, "If I start at 27 and count by tens 4 times, where will I land?" Finally, give problems in which 2 two-digit numbers are added, again encouraging counting by tens. For instance, "If I'm at square 52 and I go forward 27 squares, where will I land? What if I do the tens part of 27 first?"

You can also have students do tasks with numbered houses such as those on **STUDENT SHEET 5** ⊙ . Using the numbered houses tasks encourages students to extend their reasoning from an array context to a straight-line context. Also, the numbered houses tasks require more abstract reasoning because most of the houses are missing—so students have to use imagery or their understanding of number patterns to answer the questions. With these problems, you can ask questions similar to those you asked when you used the hundred chart. Again, the following sequence of problem types works well:

1. Add a multiple of ten to a two-digit number that is not a multiple of ten (e.g., 34 + 20).

2. Add 2 two-digit numbers that are not multiples of ten with no decade crossing or regrouping (e.g., 34 + 25).

3. Add 2 two-digit numbers that are not multiples of ten with decade crossing or regrouping (e.g., 34 + 28).

Similar sequences work well for subtraction. For instance, for 53 – 27, we might count 43, 33, 30, 26. But keep in mind that backward counting can be more difficult than forward counting.

When students are successful with visual models such as the hundred chart and house problems, encourage them to extend their counting-by-tens reasoning to symbolically represented addition and subtraction problems (e.g., 46 + 30, 35 + 53, and 48 – 34).

## Teaching Students at Level 2.2: Moving to Combining and Separating Place-Value Parts (No Skip-Counting)

The problems below encourage students to progress from counting by tens and ones to combining and separating by tens and ones without skip-counting.

1.  Deriving tens problems from basic facts.
    - "What's 40 plus 30?" If the student counts on by tens, that is good, but ask, "Is there any other way to do this problem? What is 4 plus 3? Does knowing what 4 plus 3 is help you figure out 40 plus 30?"
    - If the student needs additional help, ask, "How much is 4 groups of ten? How much is 3 groups of ten? How much is 4 groups of ten plus 3 groups of ten? What's 40 plus 30?"
    - Keep asking questions like those above, gradually adding guidance if needed.
        - "What's 50 + 40?"
        - "Does knowing what 5 plus 4 is help you figure out what 50 plus 40 is?"
        - "How much is 5 groups of ten plus 4 groups of ten?"

2.  Doing problems with place-value blocks can be useful. For instance, to have students figure out 40 plus 30 with place-value blocks, ask, "How many ten-blocks make 40? How many ten-blocks make 30? How many one-blocks are there in these 7 ten-blocks?"

    Extend both types of problems from multiples of ten to two-digit numbers that are not multiples of ten (so their ones digits are not 0). Again, increase the problem difficulty gradually:
    - Find 42 + 30, 56 + 40, and so on. [First number has tens and ones, second number has only tens.]
    - Find 42 + 35, 56 + 42, and so on. [First number has tens and ones, second number has tens and ones, no regrouping.]
    - Find 45 + 37, 56 + 48, and so on. [First number has tens and ones, second number has tens and ones, with regrouping. You might have to suggest to students (or have some of them suggest) to do the tens, then the ones, and then combine the results.]

3.  Have students do problems like those on Student Sheets 3 and 4 (tens-strips) *without counting*. (But students can count by tens to check answers.)

4.  Have students do problems mentally, without counting. **STUDENT SHEET 6** includes a variety of such problems.

## Teaching Students at Level 3: Increasing Understanding of Combining and Separating by Place Value

### Teaching Students at Level 3.1: Moving to Developing Tens Language

Problems like those on **STUDENT SHEET 7** 🔽 encourage students to use ones, tens, and hundreds language as required for Level 3.2 reasoning. For example, consider the following problem:

$$(5 \text{ tens} + 6 \text{ ones}) + (4 \text{ tens} + 3 \text{ ones}) = ?$$

Students who are operating at Level 3.2 will do this problem using tens and ones language: *5 tens plus 4 tens is 9 tens; 6 ones and 3 ones is 9 ones; 9 tens plus 9 ones is 99.* Students who are reasoning at Level 3.1 will make sense of this language by converting it into multiples of ten language. For instance, a student at Level 3.1 might do the problem as follows: *5 tens + 6 ones is 56. 4 tens + 3 ones is 43. 56 plus 40 is 96, plus 3 more is 99.*

You can encourage students who are combining and separating numbers using multiples of ten language to move to tens language by exposing them to tens language. For example, you might ask, "Let's try to make sense of another way of thinking about the problem 56 + 43." One student did the problem by saying, "5 tens plus 4 tens is 9 tens; 6 ones and 3 ones is 9 ones; 9 tens plus 9 ones is 99." What do you think of this approach? Is it the correct answer? Why did the student's way of doing the problem give the correct answer? You can also help students by having them connect the tens language to the concept of groups of ten: "What is (5 tens and 6 ones) plus (4 tens and 3 ones)? That is, what is (5 groups of ten + 6 ones) + (4 groups of ten + 3 ones)?"

If necessary, students can use place-value blocks to solve these problems. But the goal is for students to be able to do the problems without physical materials or pictures. Of course, students can always check their answers by combining using multiples of tens language or skip-counting by tens and ones. But right after they use one of these other methods, be sure to ask why the problem can also be done using tens and ones language.

### Teaching Students at Level 3.2: Moving to Developing Integrated Language and Strategy Use

Have students discuss the different strategies that can be used to add and subtract two-digit numbers. Ask questions such as, *What are the different ways that we can do the problem 42 + 34? Why do all these strategies give correct answers?* Students may suggest methods such as the following:

▦ Forty plus thirty equals seventy. Two plus four equals six. Seventy plus six equals seventy-six.

- Four tens *plus* 3 tens equals 7 tens. Two plus four equals six. Seven tens plus six equals seventy-six.
- Counting by tens and ones. Forty-two, fifty-two, sixty-two, seventy-two, seventy-six.

If you conduct enough class discussions in which students explain and reflect on the different strategies, students will come to accept all as valid, and come to see them as equivalent.

## Teaching Students at Level 3.3: Moving to Understanding Place Value in Expanded Algorithms

Before students can genuinely understand algorithms, they must be able to *mentally* combine and separate numbers by their place-value parts as in Level 3.1 through Level 3.3. Students who operate at Level 3 only when place-value blocks are available are not ready to learn algorithms for two reasons. First, they may be at a lower cognitive level when not using place-value blocks; being able to operate mentally at Level 3 is important for understanding and performing expanded algorithms.

Second, they may use the blocks in ways that are inconsistent with the algorithms. For example, when adding 26 and 38 with base-ten blocks, a student might say, "20 plus 30 is 50 (pushing 2 ten-blocks and 3 ten-blocks together), 6 plus 8 is 14 (pushing 6 one-blocks and 8 one-blocks together), 50 plus 14 is 64." This reasoning is definitely valid. *However, because the student does not regroup, this work with place-value blocks cannot serve as an appropriate mental model or justification for a traditional addition algorithm that requires regrouping.* In fact, there is no real need to regroup when using the *place-value blocks* to add numbers.

To encourage regrouping when using place-value blocks, you have to add an extra rule for using blocks—whenever there are ten of any one kind of block, you must regroup. So, a student might say, when adding 26 and 38 with base-ten blocks, "20 plus 30 is 50 *[pushing 2 ten-blocks and 3 ten-blocks together]*, 6 plus 8 is 14 *[pushing 6 one-blocks and 8 one-blocks together]*, 14 one-blocks equals 1 ten-block plus 4 one-blocks *[trading in 10 one-blocks for 1 ten-block]*; put the 1 ten-block with 5 ten-blocks and get 60, then add the 4 one-blocks to get 64."

A similar situation exists for subtraction—problems that require regrouping when using the algorithm can be solved with base-ten blocks without regrouping. For example, to find 46 minus 28 with base-ten blocks, some students say, "40 minus 20 is 20 (taking away 2 ten-blocks from 4 ten-blocks); I can't take 8 away from 6, so I take the 6 one-blocks away, then I pretend to take 2 away from the 20 (pointing at 2 ones on one of the remaining ten-blocks). There are 18 left." So again, because no regrouping is needed, although this reasoning is definitely valid, this type of reasoning with *place-value blocks cannot serve as an appropriate model for the traditional subtraction algorithm.*

Once students are able to reason at Level 3.3 without needing physical or visual material, they should be encouraged to move to expanded, conceptually explicit algorithms for addition and subtraction, as shown below. (Work on multiplication and division lags behind addition and subtraction.) These algorithms help them organize and become truly proficient in operating on two-digit numbers.

## Progressing to Expanded Addition and Subtraction Algorithms

The key to helping students learn expanded algorithms meaningfully is to guide students to see these algorithms as organized ways to implement their Level 3 reasoning. For example, consider the following discussion of the problem 342 + 435.

**Student:** *300 plus 400 equals 700; 40 plus 30 equals 70, so that's 770; 2 plus 5 equals 7, so it's 777.*

**Teacher:** *Great. I've written exactly what you said on the board. Now let's think about how we can write this strategy in an organized short way with just numbers and symbols. One way is to write it like this:*

$$300 + 40 + 2$$
$$\underline{+\ 400 + 30 + 5}$$
$$700 + 70 + 7 = 777$$

*First I broke the two numbers into their place-value parts. Then, just like you explained, I added the hundreds parts 300 plus 400, then the tens parts 40 plus 30, then the ones parts 2 plus 5. Then I added these numbers together to get the answer.*

**Teacher:** *Another way to write this procedure with just numbers and symbols is like this:*

$$342$$
$$\underline{+435}$$
$$700$$
$$70$$
$$\underline{\ \ \ 7}$$
$$777$$

**Teacher:** *Can somebody explain how this method is the same as what we said before?*

## Progressing to Expanded Multiplication and Division Algorithms

As can be seen from the expanded multiplication and division algorithms shown in Chapter 2, a critical part of using these algorithms is multiplying multiples of ten (e.g., $40 \times 30 = 1200$, $200 \times 30 = 6000$). In fact, before students can meaningfully learn expanded algorithms for multiplication and division, they must develop fluency with *mentally* multiplying multiples of 10. Problems like those below can help students understand why the "0 rule of multiplication" works (when multiplying multiples of ten, multiply the nonzero digits, then append the number of zeros that occurred in the original factors).

5 × (3 tens) = _____ tens = _____ ones

5 × 30 = _____

5 × (3 hundreds) = _____ hundreds = _____ ones

5 × 300 = _____

Students must also understand how to use the distributive property to decompose multidigit multiplication problems. Developing this understanding is difficult but critically important for understanding the algorithms and for laying the foundation for algebra. A number of ways of doing this are outlined below.

## Method 1

Have students do problems like the one below and those on **STUDENT SHEET 8** ,
perhaps starting with a problem that has one single-digit factor and one double-digit factor. (Students should be able to do the partial product calculations mentally.)

*Think about the problem 25 × 34.*

*Write the letters of the rectangles that show each product below.*

*20 × 30 = 600*    *20 × 4 = 80*    *5 × 30 = 150*    *5 × 4 = 20*

_____    _____    _____    _____

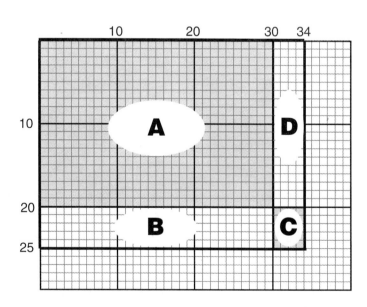

*Which products from above should be added to find the answer to 25 × 34?*

*600          80          150          20*

*Explain why your answer is correct.*

A discussion of this problem might go as follows.

*Which rectangle did you put for 20 × 30 = 600?* [A] *Why?* [Because it measures 20 units by 30 units.]

*Which rectangle did you put for 20 × 4 = 80?* [D] *Why?* [Because it measures 20 units by 4 units (34–30=4).]

*Which rectangle did you put for 5 × 30 = 150?* [B] *Why?* [Because it measures 5 units by 30 units.]

*Which rectangle did you put for 5 × 4 = 20?* [C] *Why?* [Because it measures 5 units by 4 units.]

*What is the size of the rectangle that shows 25 × 34? How is this rectangle related to rectangles A, B, C, and D?* [If you join rectangles A, B, C, and D together, you get the 25 × 34 rectangle.]

## Method 2

Students can use place-value blocks to represent place value and the distributive property as they model multiplication problems. Here are two ways to use blocks to represent the two-digit multiplication 35 × 23. Be sure that students can explain where the partial products shown in *italics* are located in the representations. For instance, you can ask, "Where is the 20 × 5?" (When students begin using this expanded symbolic algorithm, they generally write everything below the 23, just as shown below. Later, they stop writing the numbers in italics.)

$$
\begin{array}{r}
35 \\
\times 23 \\
\hline
15 \quad \text{\textit{3 × 5}} \\
90 \quad \text{\textit{3 × 30}} \\
100 \quad \text{\textit{20 × 5}} \\
\underline{600} \quad \text{\textit{20 × 30}}
\end{array}
$$

805

Note that one number is represented along the left side and the other number along the top.

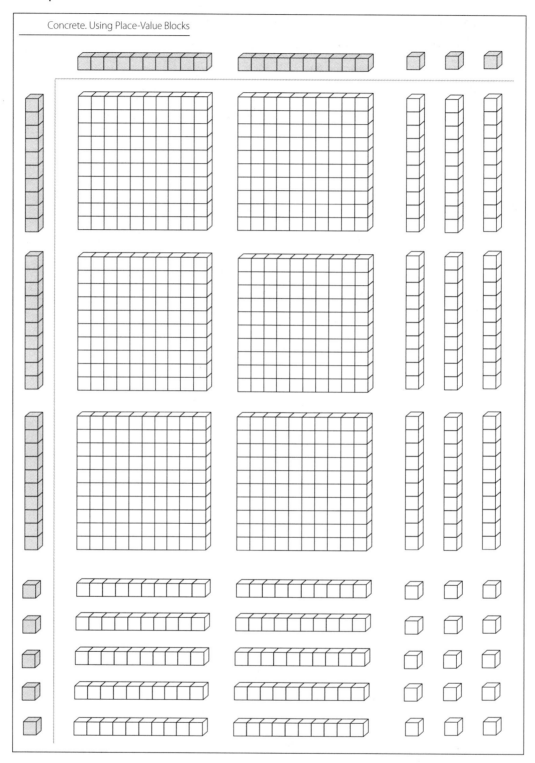

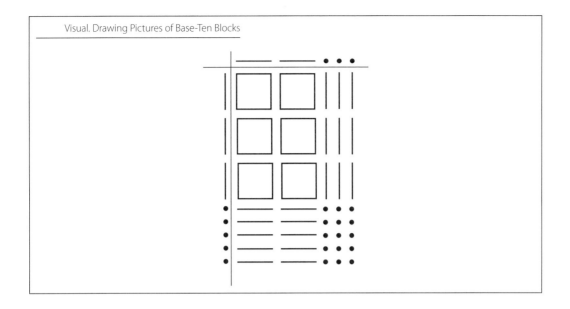

## Teaching Students at Level 4: Moving from Expanded to Traditional Algorithms

There are several ways that you can help students make sense of traditional algorithms conceptually. One way is to model the algorithm with place-value blocks (see pages 63–64 for an example). Doing steps in the base-ten block procedure *at the same time as corresponding steps* in the algorithm encourages students to develop conceptual meaning for the algorithms.

Another way is to replace the abbreviated language used in implementing traditional algorithms with conceptually explicit language. The final way, and the one that seems most meaningful to students, is to have students relate the traditional algorithms step by step to expanded algorithms with explicit place-value language.

## Replacing Abbreviated Language with Place-Value Explicit Language

| Abbreviated Language in Traditional Algorithm | Place-Value Explicit Language in Traditional Algorithm |
|---|---|
| ¹<br>46<br>+17<br>63<br><br>**S:** *6 plus 7 equals 13. Put down the 3 and carry the 1. 1 plus 4 plus 1 equals 6; write 6.* | ¹<br>46<br>+17<br>63<br><br>**S:** *6 plus 7 equals 13. Put down the 3 and bring 1 ten over to the tens column. 1 ten plus 4 tens plus 1 ten equals 6 tens or 60; write 6 in the tens column.* |

## Teaching Students at Level 4.1: Moving to Understand Traditional Algorithms for Addition and Subtraction

Again consider using the traditional algorithm on the problem 46 + 17. This problem can be done with the expanded algorithm as shown below. With both traditional and expanded algorithms visible to students, ask questions to encourage students to see precisely how the steps in the traditional algorithm correspond to steps in the expanded algorithm.

For instance, ask, "When you add 6 and 7, where do you write the 13 in the traditional algorithm, and where in the expanded algorithm? Use the expanded algorithm to explain where the 6 comes from in the traditional algorithm."

| Traditional Algorithm | Expanded Algorithm |
|---|---|
| $\overset{1}{4}6$ <br> $+17$ <br> $63$ <br><br> **S:** *6 plus 7 equals 13. Put down the 3 and carry the 1. 1 plus 4 plus 1 equals 6; write 6.* | $\overset{1}{4}6$ <br> $+17$ <br> $13$ <br> $\underline{50}$ <br> $63$ <br><br> **S:** *6 plus 7 equals 13. 40 plus 10 equals 50. 50 plus 10 from the 13 equals 60. 60 plus 3 equals 63.* |

A similar connection can be made between the traditional subtraction algorithm and an expanded subtraction algorithm.

| | | |
|---|---|---|
| $\overset{3}{}\overset{1}{4}6$ <br> $-17$ <br> $29$ | $40 + 6 \longrightarrow$ <br> $-(10 + 7)$ | $30 + 16$ <br> $-(10 + \phantom{0}7)$ <br> $20 + \phantom{0}9 = 29$ |
| **S:** *You can't take 7 from 6, so you have to borrow 1 from the 4 to make 16. 16 − 7 = 9. 3 − 1 = 2. 29.* | **S:** *[Rewrites 46 as 40 + 6; 17 as 10 + 7.]* <br> *You can't take 7 from 6, so you have to take 10 from the 40 and add it to 6 to make 16.* | **S:** *16 − 7 = 9. 30 − 10 = 20. 20 + 9 = 29.* |

## Teaching Students at Level 4.2: Moving to Understanding Traditional Algorithms for Multiplication

The traditional algorithm for multiplying these two numbers is shown below. The language the student uses in performing this algorithm does not make the place values of digits evident. Place value is dealt with by the *positioning* of digits in partial products.

**Task:** *45 × 23 =* _____

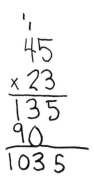

**Student:** [As he writes] *3 times 5 is 15, write the 5, put the 1 up here* [writes 1 above 4]. *3 times 4 is 12, plus 1 is 13* [writes 13]. *2 times 5 is 10, write the 0, put the 1 up here* [writing 0 below the 3 in the first partial product and the 1 above and to the left of the 4]. *2 times 4 is 8 plus 1 is 9.*

The traditional algorithm reduces the problem of multiplying multidigit numbers to operating on *single digits* by using basic multiplication facts (a one-digit number times a one-digit number) and appropriate spatial positioning of the digits in the results. However, even though this spatial positioning is determined by place value, it is usually not explicitly mentioned while performing the algorithm.

The expanded algorithms shown below make the manipulations of place value parts and steps explicit.

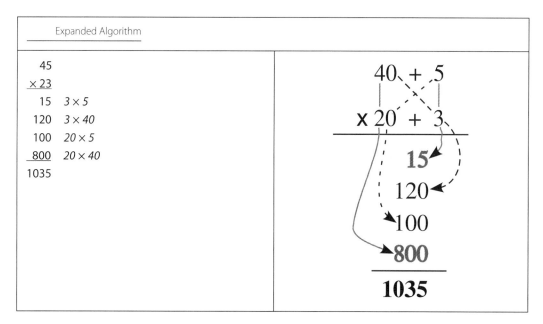

To help students understand the traditional algorithm, guide them to relate the steps in the traditional algorithm to corresponding steps in the expanded algorithm, as illustrated below. If students have difficulty understanding this connection in multiplying a two-digit number by a two-digit number, try it with multiplying a two-digit number by a one-digit number.

**Teacher:** *Use the problem on the left to explain where the numbers come from in the problem on the right.*

---

Expanded and Traditional Algorithms

$$
\begin{array}{r}
45 \\
\times\ 23 \\
\hline
15 \\
120 \\
100 \\
800 \\
\hline
1035
\end{array}
\qquad
\begin{array}{r}
45 \\
\times\ 23 \\
\hline
135 \\
90 \\
\hline
1035
\end{array}
$$

---

**Student:** *The 135 here* [Traditional] *comes from the 120 + 15 here* [Expanded].

**Teacher:** *And where do the 120 and 15 come from?*

**Student:** *From multiplying 45 times 3; 45 is 40 + 5.*

**Teacher:** *Where does the 90 in the traditional algorithm come from?*

**Student:** *It's 90 tens, so it really means 900. It comes from the 100 + 800 in the expanded algorithm.*

**Teacher:** *Where do the 100 and 800 come from?*

**Student:** *From multiplying 45 times the 20 in 23 because 45 equals 40 + 5.*

Another opportunity to help students understand traditional algorithms arises when students make place-value related mistakes with the algorithms.

---

*Problem.* $45 \times 34 =$ _____

**Student:** 5 times 4 equals 20. 5 times 3 equals 15. 4 times 3 equals 12. 4 times 4 equals 16. Add it up and you get 63.

**Teacher:** What does the 3 in 34 mean? Is it 3 or 30?

**Student:** It's 30.

**Teacher:** Does that change your answer?

**Student:** I guess I should have multiplied 5 times 30, so my answer is wrong.

**Teacher:** *[Pointing to the 4 in 45]* What does this number mean? Is it 4 or 40? Does that change your answer?

**Student:** I think it's 40.

**Teacher:** So let's try to do this problem together . . . .

$$
\begin{array}{r}
34 \\
\times\ 45 \\
\hline
\overset{1}{2}0 \\
15 \\
12 \\
16 \\
\hline
6\,3
\end{array}
$$

## Teaching Students at Level 4.2: Moving to Understand Traditional Algorithms for Division

Consider the three methods for solving the same division problem shown below. Methods 1 and 2 are different implementations of an expanded algorithm; Method 3 is an implementation of a traditional algorithm.

| Method 1 Conceptually Explicit or Expanded Algorithm | Method 2 Conceptually Explicit or Expanded Algorithm | Method 3 Traditional Algorithm |
|---|---|---|
| $4\overline{)928}$ <br> $-400$  $-(100 \times 4)$ <br> $528$ <br> $-400$  $-(100 \times 4)$ <br> $128$ <br> $-40$  $-(10 \times 4)$ <br> $88$ <br> $-80$  $-(20 \times 4)$ <br> $8$ <br> $-8$  $-(2 \times 4)$ <br> $0$  $232$ <br><br> Answer: 232 | $4\overline{)928}$ <br> $-800$  $-(200 \times 4)$ <br> $128$ <br> $-120$  $-(30 \times 4)$ <br> $8$ <br> $-8$  $-(2 \times 4)$ <br> $0$  $232$ <br><br> Answer: 232 | $232$ <br> $4\overline{)928}$ <br> $-8$ <br> $12$ <br> $-12$ <br> $08$ <br> $-8$ <br> $0$ |

Both the expanded and traditional algorithms can be interpreted as determining how many times 4 can be subtracted from 928 or how many 4s are in 928.

In Method 1, the student uses familiar landmarks to determine how many 4s to subtract at each stage. The total number of times 4 is subtracted from 928 is gotten by adding the partial quotients: $100 + 100 + 10 + 20 + 2$.

In Method 2, the student maximizes the partial quotients by using place value to determine how many times 4 can be subtracted from 928.

**Step 1.** How many hundreds of times can I subtract 4 from 928? If I subtract four 100 times, that's 400, which is less than 928. If I subtract four 200 times, that's 800, which is still less than 928. If I subtract four 300 times, that's 1200, which is more than 928, so 300 is too many times. So I should subtract four 200 times. Subtract 800 from 928 and you get 128 left.

**Step 2.** How many tens of times can I subtract 4 from 128? 10 times, that's 40; 20 times, that's 80; 30 times, that's 120; 40 times would be too much. So it's 30 times. Subtract 120 from 128 and you have 8 left.

**Step 3.** How many times can I subtract 4 from 8? 1 time would be 4, 2 times would be 8. The total number of times 4 is subtracted from 928 is thus $200 + 30 + 2$.

You can help students connect the expanded and traditional algorithms by asking appropriate questions.

**Teacher:** *Can you use Method 2 to explain where the numbers are coming from in Method 3?*

**Student:** *The numbers match up. This 2 here in Method 3* [pointing to the quotient] *is the 200 in Method 2. The 3 is the 30, and the last 2 is just the 2. And the first minus 8* [in Method 3] *is the minus 800 over here* [Method 2]; *the minus 12 is the minus 120 over here, and the minus 8 is the minus 8 over here.*

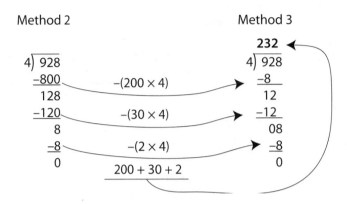

**Teacher:** *Why is the 2 in Method 3 the same as the 200 in Method 2?*

**Student:** *Method 2 says that 4 can be subtracted from 928 two hundred times. In Method 3, when you say that there are two 4s in 9, you mean that the number of hundred times that you can subtract 4 from 9 hundred is 2.*

## Teaching Students at Level 5: Moving to Understanding Larger Numbers, Numbers Less than 1, and Exponential Notation

As explained in Chapter 2, to move to Level 6, students deepen and extend their understanding of number naming schemes, of relationships between place values, and of the exponential format for expressing numbers as a sum of their place-value parts.

### Understanding Place Value in Large Numbers

After explaining the Place-Value Chart for Whole Numbers (see Chapter 2, page 39) and showing a couple of examples, have students use the chart to do problems like those on **STUDENT SHEET 9** . For example, use the chart to explain that the name for 465,483,579 is *four-hundred sixty-five million, four-hundred eighty-three thousand, five-hundred seventy-nine*, and that the 6 in this number has value 6 ten-millions, and the 8 has value 8 ten-thousands.

One activity that is useful for helping students deepen their understanding of place value is to use a calculator to solve the following type of problem:

*Enter 1234444.567 on your calculator. What number do I have to subtract to change the 3 to a 0? What number do I have to subtract to change the 6 to a 0?*

Students reasoning at Level 1 are most likely to subtract 3 and 6. Students at Level 6 are more likely to subtract 30000 and .06. Students at Level 3 and above can start making sense of such problems if a smaller whole number is entered into the calculator:

*Enter 1234 on your calculator. What number do I have to subtract to change the 3 to a 0?*

Another part of understanding place value at Level 6 is being able to construct a number given its place-value parts, as in Task Sets 1 and 2 below.

## Task Set 1

*9 ten-thousands + 8 hundreds + 3 ones = _____*

*52 thousands + 32 hundreds + 5 = _____*

*32,000 – thirty thousand = _____*

If students have difficulties with Task Set 1, try rephrasing the problems using "groups of" language. For example, the first problem could be rephrased as: "9 groups of ten-thousand + 8 groups of one hundred + 3 ones = _____." Also, allow students to write their answers in several ways. For instance, for 2 thousands – 8 hundreds, they could write "1 thousand + 2 hundreds" or, in standard form, 1,200. Using both expressions helps develop deeper understanding of the standard form.

## Task Set 2

**SEQUENCE A**

*1 thousand – 8 hundreds = _____*

*2 thousands – 8 hundreds = _____*

*3 thousands – 8 hundreds = _____*

*24 thousands – 8 hundreds = _____*

**SEQUENCE B**

*1 million – 700 thousands = _____*

*2 millions – 700 thousands = _____*

*7 millions – 700 thousands = _____*

## Decimals Less Than 1

One way you can encourage students to construct meaning for decimal numbers that are less than 1 is by giving them problems that require them to relate decimal numbers to their place-value parts. For example, the problem below requires students to see how the decimal parts of the number 53 hundredths (5 tenths, 3 hundredths) are related to the number (53 hundredths).

**Task:** *5 tenths + 3 hundredths = _____ hundredths.*

**Response:** 5 tenths = 50 hundredths because 5/10 = 50/100.
So 5 tenths + 3 hundredths = 50 hundredths + 3 hundredths = 53 hundredths.

Another way you can encourage students to construct meaning for decimal numbers that are less than 1 is by giving them problems that encourage them to relate decimal numbers to their fraction equivalents. For example, in the problem below ask students to use fractions to show why 5 tenths + 3 hundredths = 53 hundredths.

**Task:** *Show why 5 tenths + 3 hundredths = 53 hundredths.*

**Response:**

$$5 \text{ tenths} + 3 \text{ hundredths} = \frac{5}{10} + \frac{3}{100} = \frac{50}{100} + \frac{3}{100} = \frac{53}{100} = 53 \text{ hundredths}$$

After explaining the Place-Value Chart for Numbers Less Than 1 (see Chapter 2, page 39) and showing a couple of examples, have students use the chart to do problems like those on **STUDENT SHEET 10** ⬇ . For example, use the chart to explain that the name for .465483 is *four-hundred sixty-five thousand, four-hundred eighty-three millionths*, and that the 6 in this number has value 6 hundredths, and the 8 has value 8 hundred-thousandths.

**Task:** *Tell the value of each 2 in the number 2222.222.*

**Response:** Going from left to right:

*The first 2 has value 2000.*

*The second 2 has value 200.*

*The third 2 has value 20.*

*The fourth 2 has value 2.*

*The fifth 2 has value 2/10.*

*The sixth 2 has value 2/100.*

*The seventh 2 has value 2/1000.*

To encourage students to better understand the relationship between different place values, give problems like those on **STUDENT SHEETS 11** (whole numbers) and **12** (fractions) ⬇ . For instance, in the problem, A number has a 3 in its tens place. When the number is multiplied by 10, what place is the 3 in? students first predict an answer, then check it on a calculator by entering a number with a 3 in the tens place and multiplying by 10. For example, students might enter 135, then predict where the 3 will be when they multiply it by ten (in the hundreds place). Students who understand the relationship between different place values will be able to predict the

## Place-Value Chart for Numbers Less Than 1

| Place Value | ones | . | tenths | hundredths | thousandths | ten-thousandths | hundred-thousandths | millionths |
|---|---|---|---|---|---|---|---|---|
| Place-Value Number | 1 | | .1 = 1/10 | .01 = 1/100 | .001 = 1/1000 | .0001 = 1/10000 | .00001 = 1/100000 | .000001 = 1/1000000 |
| Example | | . | 4 | 6 | 5 | 4 | 8 | 3 |

answer correctly without calculators. Students who don't understand the relationship may have to try several problems on a calculator before understanding the answer.

## Moving to Exponential Notation for Place Value Parts

Understanding exponential notation of place-value parts includes (a) understanding exponential notation, and (b) explicitly seeing that moving from one digit to the next digit to the left multiplies the digit's value by ten, whereas moving from one digit to next digit to the right divides the digit's value by ten.

Because exponential notation is a symbolic convention, you should show students what it means, using many examples.

### Definitions

- If X and Y are positive integers, then $X^Y$ means to multiply X together Y times. For example, $5^4 = 5 \times 5 \times 5 \times 5 = 625$
- If X and Y are positive integers, then $X^{-Y} = 1/X^Y$. For example, $5^{-2} = 1/5^2 = 1/25$
- If X is a positive integer, then $X^0 = 1$. For example, $5^0 = 1$

**Task:** *Use the definitions of exponents to find the values of powers of ten below. How are these powers of ten related to place value?*

$10^3 =$ _____ *[Response: $= 10 \times 10 \times 10 = 1000$]*

$10^2 =$ _____ *[Response: $= 10 \times 10 = 100$]*

$10^1 =$ _____ *[Response: $= 10$]*

$10^0 =$ _____ *[Response: $= 1$]*

$10^{-1} =$ _____ *[Response: $= 1/10$]*

$10^{-2} =$ _____ *[Response: $= 1/10^2 = 1/100$]*

$10^{-3} =$ _____ *[Response: $= 1/10^3 = 1/1000$]*

**Task:** *Write 2222.222 in expanded form with and without exponents.*

**Responses:**

$2222.222 = 2000 + 200 + 20 + 2 + 2/10 + 2/100 + 2/1000$

$= 2 \times (1000) + 2 \times (100) + 2 \times (10) + 2 + 2 \times (1/10) + 2 \times (1/100) + 2 \times (1/1000)$

$= 2 \times (10^3) + 2 \times (10^2) + 2 \times (10^1) + 2(10^0) + 2 \times (10^{-1}) + 2 \times (10^{-2}) + 2 \times (10^{-3})$

Students must learn many additional ideas related to decimal numbers. For instance, students must learn how to perform the four arithmetic operations on decimal numbers. Although these additional ideas are beyond the scope of CBA, getting students proficient with Level 6 reasoning will prepare them for learning these additional ideas with deep understanding.

# Appendix

## CBA Assessment Tasks for Place Value

These problems can be used in individual interviews with children or in class as instructional activities. No matter which use you choose, it is critical to get the students to write and describe or discuss their strategies. Only then can you use the CBA levels to interpret students' responses and decide on needed instruction.

## Guide for Interviewing Students with CBA Tasks

The purpose of interviewing students with CBA tasks is to determine how they are reasoning and, more specifically, to determine what CBA levels of reasoning they are using for the tasks. Here is what CBA staff said to students before the interviews:

> I am going to give you some problems. I would like to know what you think while you solve these problems. So, tell me everything you think as you do the problems. Try to think out loud. Tell me what you are doing and why you are doing it. I will also ask you questions to help me understand what you are thinking. For instance, if you say something that I don't understand, I will ask you questions about it.

If you don't understand what a student is saying, you could say, "I don't understand, could you explain that again?" or "What do you mean by such-and-such?" Try to get students to explain in their own words rather than paraphrasing what you think they mean and asking if they agree. If, during an interview, a student asked whether his or her answers are correct, we told the student that, for this interview, it does not really matter. We are interested in what he or she thinks.

Students responded to our request to "think out loud" in two ways. Many students were quite capable of thinking out loud as they solved problems. They told us what they were thinking and doing as they thought about and did it. Other students, however, seemed unable to think aloud as they completed problems. They worked in silence, but then gave us detailed accounts of what they did *after* they finished doing it.

The following tasks cover a large range of reasoning about place value. You probably will not want to give all the problems to your students, at least not at one time. We suggest using Problems 1–6 for students in Grades 1 and 2, Problems 3–8 for students in Grades 3–5, and Problems 9–12 in Grades 4–5. Of course, you can alter these suggestions based on your curriculum.

Many of the problems have notes that indicate particular aspects of students' reasoning emphasized by the problems.

Additional assessment tasks (including more tasks appropriate for Grades 4–5) may be downloaded from this book's website, www.heinemann.com/products/E04343.aspx (click on the "Companion Resources" tab).

## Teacher Notes for Individual Tasks

**Problem 2.** The problem is presented in three parts using either the CBA student sheet or on a projector. For parts (b) and (c), it is critical to determine how students are counting: by ones only, by tens and ones separately, or by counting by tens in mid-decades.

(a) Use an overhead projector or document camera and an opaque piece of paper or cardboard to cover the diagram as shown below.

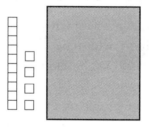

Say, "Here is a strip of 10 squares and some single squares. How many squares are there altogether?"

(b) Uncover additional squares as shown below.

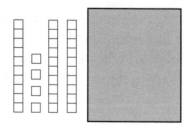

Say, "How many squares are there altogether?"

(c) Uncover additional squares as shown below.

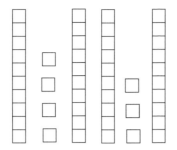

Say, "How many squares are there altogether?"

**Problem 7.** Many students interpret the equal sign as a command to do the computation shown on the left of the sign instead of as a statement of equivalence of two quantities. This is one reason a student might write 53 in the first blank for this problem. If you suspect that a student is using this misinterpretation, you might pose Problem 7 in a different way:

*5 tens and 3 ones = 13 ones and _____ tens*

Or you might say, "What do I have to put in the blank space so that 13 ones and _____ tens is the same amount as 5 tens and 3 ones?"

If students need more help with the correct interpretation of the equal sign, it will be helpful to discuss with students how a statement that uses the equal sign can be interpreted as being in balance on a balance scale (or even a teeter totter).

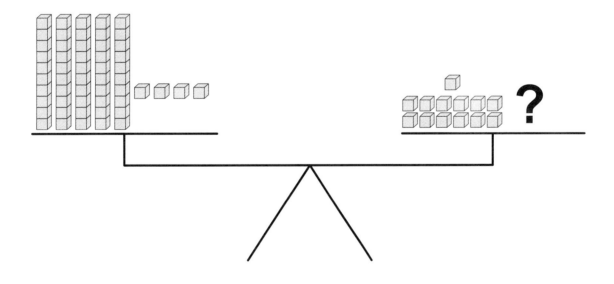

Name _____     Date _____

This assessment is to be given to students orally, with a few more than 30 cubes available.

**0.** Can you give me 5 cubes?

Can you give me 8 cubes?

Can you give me 14 cubes?

Can you give me 23 cubes?

Name _____    Date _____

**1.** Jon has 30 checkers. How many stacks of ten checkers can he make?

Name _____    Date _____

**2.** (a)  Here is a strip of 10 squares and some single squares.

How many squares are there altogether?                                                Answer _____

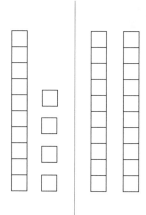

(b)  How many squares are there altogether?                                            Answer _____

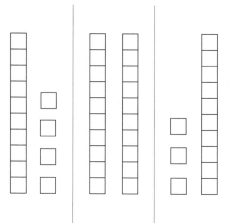

(c)  How many squares are there altogether?                                            Answer _____

**3.** There are 37 squares under the circle.
There are also 2 ten-strips of squares and 5 single squares.
How many squares are there altogether?

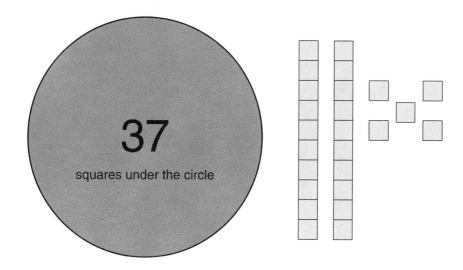

37

squares under the circle

**4.** On a street, there are 100 buildings. There is room to show only 30 buildings on this page.

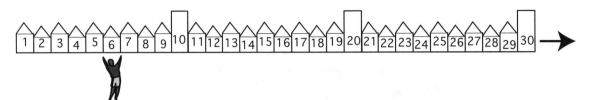

(a) If I'm at building 6 and I go forward 1 building, where am I?

(b) If I'm at building 6 and I go forward 10 buildings, where am I?

(c) If I'm at building 6 and I go forward 30 buildings, where am I?

**5.** In a box, there are 35 red apples and 27 green apples.

How many apples are in the box?

**6.** $60 + 8 = $ _____ tens and _____ ones.

**7.** 5 tens and 3 ones = 13 ones and _____ tens.

**8.** (50 and 13) − (30 and 8) = _____.

Name _____     Date _____

**9.** 9 thousands + 8 hundreds + 3 = _____.

**10.** 5 × (3 tens) = _____ ones.

**11.** 2 hundreds = _____ tens.
5 thousands = _____ hundreds = _____ tens.
1 thousand – 8 hundreds = _____.

**12.** 2 thousands – 8 hundreds = _____.
3 thousands – 8 hundreds = _____.
24 thousands – 8 hundreds = _____.
1 million = _____ thousands.

# CBA Levels for Each Task

The descriptions below show sample student responses at various levels of sophistication.

## PROBLEM 0

Can you give me 5 cubes? Can you give me 8 cubes? Can you give me 14 cubes? Can you give me 23 cubes? *[With a few more than 30 cubes available.]*

**Level 0:** The student has difficulty counting the given number of checkers.

**Levels 1–6:** The student correctly counts the given number of checkers.

## PROBLEM 1

Jon has 30 checkers. How many stacks of ten checkers can he make? *[With a few more than 30 cubes available.]*

**Level 0:** The student has difficulty counting 30 checkers.

**Level 1.1:** The student correctly counts 30 checkers but cannot determine that there are 3 stacks of ten.

**Level 1.2:** The student divides 30 checkers into 3 groups and correctly says that there are 3 stacks of ten checkers.

**Level 1.3:** Student says "30 is 3 ten-blocks *[using place-value blocks]*." When asked how many checkers are in 3 stacks of ten, the student counts the individual cubes on the 3 ten-blocks.

**Level 2.1:** Student says "10, 20, 30 *[perhaps putting up 3 fingers]*, there are 3 stacks of ten."

**Level 2.2:** Not applicable.

**Level 3.1:** The student says that 30 is 3 tens and can explain why. For instance, the student might say 30 is 10, 20, 30 *[putting up 3 fingers successively]*, so there are 3 tens.

**Level 3.2:** The student says that 30 is 3 tens and can explain why. For instance the student might say that if you put 3 tens or groups of ten together, you get 30.

**Levels 4–6:** Not applicable.

## PROBLEM 2

*[Note carefully how students count when doing this problem.]*

**Level 0:** Student has difficulty counting squares by ones.

**Levels 1.1–1.2:** Student correctly counts all squares by ones.

**Level 1.3:** Student says, in (b), "there are 3 tens, which is 30" (but can't explain why), then counts on from 30; 31, 32, 33, 34; or counts 14 by ones, then on the next ten-strip counts by ones, 15, 16, . . . , 23, 24, *[then by the ones on the next strip]*, 25, 26, . . . , 33, 34.

**Level 2.1:** In (b), student says, "10, 20, 30" *[while pointing to the strips]*, then says "31, 32, 33, 34" (or just says 34).

**Level 2.2:** In (b), student skip-counts 10, 14, 24, 34 *[while pointing to strips and singles]*.

**Level 3.1:** In (c), student says, "you add the tens—ten plus twenty plus ten equals forty—then add the ones, 4 + 3 = 7, so that makes 47."

**Level 3.2:** In (c), student says, "1 ten plus 2 tens plus 1 ten equals 4 tens, plus 7, equals 47."

**Levels 4–6:** Not applicable.

## PROBLEM 3

There are 37 squares under the circle. There are also 2 ten-strips of squares and 5 single squares. How many squares are there altogether?

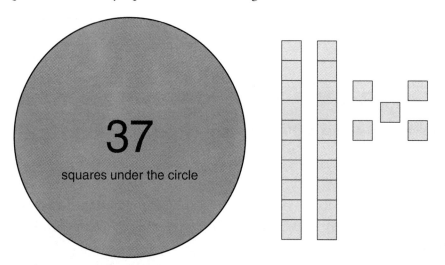

Note. If a student counts the squares in one of the ten-strips (1, 2, . . . , 10), that does not affect the determination of level.

**Level 0:** Student has difficulty counting squares by ones.

**Levels 1.1–1.2:** Student correctly counts squares by ones, starting at 37.

**Level 1.3:** Student uses traditional algorithm rotely to add 37 and 25 but can't explain where the "carried" 1 comes from when adding 7 and 5; or uses place-value blocks to do the problem. That is, student gets 5 ten-strip and 12 ones, then counts by ones: 50, 51, 52, . . . , 62.

**Level 2.1:** Student says, "10, 20, 30" *[while pointing to the circle]*, then says, "40, 50, 57, 58, 59, 60, 61, 62."

**Level 2.2:** Student skip-counts 37, 47, 57, 60, 62 *[or counts last 5 by ones, or adds 5 to 57 to get 62 directly]*.

**Level 3.1:** Student says, "30 plus 20 is 50; 7 plus 5 is 12, 50 plus 12 is 62."

**Level 3.2:** Student says, "3 tens plus 2 tens is 5 tens; 7 plus 5 is 12, which is 1 ten and 2 ones. So 6 tens and 2 ones is 62."

**Level 4:** Student uses expanded algorithm to add 37 and 25.

**Level 5:** Student uses traditional algorithm to add 37 and 25 and can explain the algorithm.

**Level 6:** Not applicable.

## PROBLEM 4

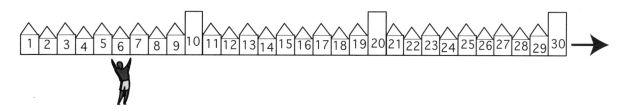

(a) If I'm at building 6 and I go forward 1 building, where am I?
(b) If I'm at building 6 and I go forward 10 buildings, where am I?
(c) If I'm at building 6 and I go forward 30 buildings, where am I?

**Level 0:** Student has difficulty counting houses by ones.

**Level 1.1:** The student uses counting by ones to correctly find answers to (a) and (b), but is unable to find the answer to (c) because some houses at the end are missing.

**Levels 1.2–1.3:** Not applicable.

**Level 2.1:** For (b), student says, "10, 16." Or, "10, 11, 12, 13, 14, 15, 16."
For (c), student says, "10, 20, 30, 36." Or, "10, 20, 30, 31, 32, 33, 34, 35, 36."

**Level 2.2:** For (b), student says, "6, 16."
For (c), student says, "6, 16, 26, 36."

**Level 3.1:** For (b), student says, "six plus ten equals sixteen."
For (c), student says, "six plus thirty equals thirty-six."

**Level 3.2:** For (b), student says, "6 plus 1 ten equals 16."
For (c), student says, "6 plus 3 tens equals 36."

**Levels 4–6:** Not applicable.

## PROBLEM 5

In a box, there are 35 red apples and 27 green apples. How many apples are in the box?

**Level 0:** Student has difficulty counting by ones *[counting counters, circles for apples, or even numerals 1–62].*

**Level 1.1:** Student correctly counts by ones to find the sum.

**Level 1.2:** Not applicable.

**Level 1.3:** Student uses traditional algorithm rotely to add 35 and 27 but can't explain where the "carried" 1 comes from when adding 7 and 5; or makes the mistake shown below; or uses place-value blocks to do the problem but counts by ones to find the sum.

$$\begin{array}{r} 35 \\ +27 \\ \hline 512 \end{array}$$

**Level 2.1:** Student counts, 10, 20, 30, 40, 50, 51, 52, 53, 54, 55, 56, 57, 58, 59, 60, 61, 62.

**Level 2.2:** Student skip-counts, 35, 45, 55, 56, 57, 58, 59, 60, 61, 62.

**Level 3.1:** Student says, "30 + 20 = 50, 5 + 7 = 12, 50 + 12 = 62."

**Level 3.2:** Student says, "3 tens + 2 tens = 5 tens; 5 + 7 = 1 ten + 2 ones; 5 tens + 1 ten = 6 tens + 2 ones = 62."

**Level 4:** Student uses expanded algorithm.

**Level 5:** Student uses the traditional algorithm with understanding.

**Level 6:** Not applicable.

## PROBLEM 6

$$60 + 8 = \underline{\hspace{1cm}} \text{ tens and } \underline{\hspace{1cm}} \text{ ones.}$$

**Level 0:** Not applicable.

**Level 1.1:** Student answers, "60 tens and 8 ones."

**Level 1.2:** Student uses place-value blocks or physical counters to find that 60 is 6 groups of ten.

**Level 1.3:** Student says, "60 + 8 = 68; just put 6 in tens and 8 in ones."

**Level 2.1:** Student counts, "10, 20, 30, 40, 50, 60 *[using fingers to keep track]*; that's 6 tens; 8 is 8 ones."

**Level 2.2:** Student skip-counts, 18, 28, 38, 48, 58, 68 *[putting 1 finger up for each count]*, 6 tens; 8 ones.

**Level 3.1:** Student says, "Sixty is 6 tens and eight is 8 ones."

**Level 3.2:** Student says, "6 is in the tens place in 60, so there are 6 tens. And 0 + 8 ones equals 8."

**Levels 4–6:** Not applicable.

## PROBLEM 7

5 tens and 3 ones = 13 ones and _____ tens.

**Level 0:** Not applicable.

**Level 1.1:** Student says, "13 ones and 50 tens."

**Level 1.2:** Student uses place-value blocks.

**Level 1.3:** Student says, "Just put 5 for tens."

**Level 2.1:** Student says, "5 tens and 3 ones is 53. If I have 13 ones, that's 10; 20, 30, 40, 50 *[raising 4 fingers]*; so it's 4 tens."

**Level 2.2:** Student skip-counts, 13; 23, 33, 43, 53 *[raising 4 fingers]*; so it's 4 tens.

**Level 3.1:** Student says, "Ten (from 13) + forty = fifty. Forty is 4 tens."

**Level 3.2:** Student says, "1 ten in 13 + 4 tens makes 5 tens in fifty."

**Level 4.1:** Student uses an expanded algorithm to show that 53 – 13 = 40, then says that 40 is 4 tens.

**Levels 4.2–4.6:** Not applicable.

## PROBLEM 8

(50 and 13) – (30 and 8) = _____.

**Level 0:** Student counts down from 63 incorrectly by ones.

**Level 1.1:** Student counts down by ones to find 63 – 38; or student counts on by ones from 38 to 63.

**Level 1.2:** Not applicable.

**Level 1.3:** Student rotely uses algorithm to find 63 – 38; uses place-value blocks to do the problem but counts by ones to find what's left after taking away 38; or gets 5 ten-blocks and 13 ones, removes 3 ten-blocks and 8 ones, and counts by ones, 20, 21, 22, . . . , 25.

**Level 2.1:** Student counts backwards: 50; 40, 30, that's 20. 13; 12, 11, 10, 9, 8 *[putting up fingers]*; that's 5. So 25; or counts up by tens: 30; 40, 50, that's 20. 8; 9, 10, 11, 12, 13 *[putting up fingers]*; that's 5. So 25.

**Level 2.2:** Student counts down: "63; 53, 43; that's 20. 43; 42, 41, 40, 39, 38 *[putting up fingers]*; that's 5. So 25"; or skip-counts up: 38; 48, 58, that's 20. Add 2, makes 60; add 3, makes 63; that's 5. So 25.

**Level 3.1:** Student says, "fifty – thirty = 20, thirteen – eight = five, twenty + five = twenty-five."

**Level 3.2:** Student says, "5 tens – 3 tens = 2 tens, 13 – 8 = 5, 2 tens and 5 is 25."

**Level 4:** Student uses and writes an expanded algorithm.

$$
\begin{array}{r}
50 + 13 \\
-\ 30 - 8 \\
\hline
20 + 5 = 25
\end{array}
$$

**Level 5:** Student uses the traditional algorithm with understanding.

**Level 6:** Not applicable.

## PROBLEM 9

9 thousands + 8 hundreds + 3 = _____.

**Levels 0–1.2:** Not applicable.

**Level 1.3:** Student adds, 9 + 8 + 3 = 20.

**Levels 2–5:** Not applicable.

**Level 6:** Student translates given number into the appropriate numeral, 9803, and explains the place value of each digit: 9 thousands, 8 hundreds, 0 tens, 3 ones.

## PROBLEM 10

5 × (3 tens) = _____ ones.

**Level 0:** Student tries to do the problem 5 × 3 by making 5 groups of 3 cubes, but makes mistakes in counting cubes by ones.

**Levels 1.1–1.2:** Not applicable.

**Level 1.3:** Student treats the problem as 5 × 3 by making 5 groups of 3 cubes, or even 5 groups of 3 tens-blocks, but gets an answer of 15.

**Level 2.1:** Student counts 15 tens—10, 20, 30; 40, 50, 60; . . . 130, 140, 150. Could use place-value blocks or *[more sophisticated]* raising a finger for each ten counted.

**Level 2.2:** Not applicable.

**Level 3.1:** Student says, "3 tens equals 30, and 5 times 30 is 150."

**Level 3.2:** Student says, "5 times 3 tens equals 15 tens, and 15 tens is 10 tens, which is 100, plus 5 tens or 50, so it equals 150."

**Level 3.3** Not applicable.

**Level 4:** Student uses and writes an expanded algorithm:

5 times 30 is 150.

```
   30
 × 5
  150
```

**Level 5:** Student uses a traditional algorithm with understanding:

5 times 0 is 0; 5 times 3 is 15; so 150 is the answer. *[But student can explain why he used these steps using place-value concepts.]*

```
   30
 × 5
    0
   15
  150
```

**Level 6:** Not applicable.


## PROBLEM 11

**2 hundreds = _____ tens.**

**Levels 0–1:** Student says he or she does not know or answers 200.

**Level 2.1:** Student says, "Two hundreds = 200; 10, 20, 30, 40, . . . ,100; 110, 120, 130, 140, . . . , 200; that's 20 tens."

**Level 2.2:** Student skip-counts 1 ten is 10, 2 tens is 20, . . . , 19 tens is 190, 20 tens is 200.

**Level 3.1:** Not applicable.

**Level 3.2:** Student says, "1 hundred is 10 tens. 2 hundreds is 20 tens."

**Level 4:** Student uses expanded algorithm to divide 200 by 10 to get 20.

**Level 5:** Student uses traditional algorithm to divide 200 by 10 to get 20.

**Level 6:** Student says, "2 hundreds, multiply by ten to get the number of tens, so it's 20 tens."

**5 thousands = _____ hundreds = _____ tens.**

**Levels 0–1:** Student says he or she does not know or answers 5000.

**Level 2.1:** *[Writing tally marks on paper for each 100.]* Student skip-counts 100, 200, . . . , 5000. I count 50 marks. *[Can't find the number of tens.]*

**Level 2.2:** *[Writing tally marks on paper for each 100.]* Student says, "1 hundred is 100, 2 hundreds is 200, . . . , 50 hundreds is 5000. I count 50 marks." *[Can't find the number of tens.]*

**Level 3.1:** Not applicable.

**Level 3.2:** Student says, "10 hundreds = 1000, multiply by 5, so 50 hundreds = 5000. There's 10 tens in 1 hundred, so there's 50 times 10 tens, which is 500 tens, in 5000."

**Level 4:** Student uses expanded algorithm to divide 5000 by 100, and divide 5000 by 10.

**Level 5:** Student uses traditional algorithm with understanding to divide 5000 by 100, and divide 5000 by 10.

**Level 6:** Student says, "5 thousands, multiply by 10 to get the number of hundreds, so it's 50 hundreds," or "5 thousands, multiply by 100 to get the number of tens, so it's 500 tens; you multiply by 100 to move from thousands to tens."

**1 thousand – 8 hundreds = _____.**

**Levels 0–1.2:** Not applicable.

**Level 1.3:** Student uses the traditional algorithm rotely.

$$\begin{array}{r} 1{,}000 \\ -\ 800 \\ \hline 200 \end{array}$$

**Levels 2–4:** Not applicable.

**Level 5:** Student uses the traditional algorithm with understanding.

$$\begin{array}{r} 1000 \\ -\ 800 \\ \hline 200 \end{array}$$

**Level 6:** Student says, "1 thousand = 10 hundreds; 10 hundreds – 8 hundreds = 2 hundreds."

## PROBLEM 12

**2 thousands – 8 hundreds = _____.**

**Levels 1–4:** Not applicable.

**Level 5:** Student uses the traditional algorithm with understanding.

$$\begin{array}{r} 2000 \\ -\ 800 \\ \hline 200 \end{array}$$

**Level 6:** Student says, "2 thousands = 20 hundreds; 20 hundreds – 8 hundreds = 12 hundreds = 1200."

**3 thousands – 8 hundreds = _____.**

**Levels 0–4:** Not applicable.

**Level 5:** Student uses the traditional algorithm with understanding.

```
 3000
 −800
 2200
```

**Level 6:** Student says, "3 thousands = 30 hundreds; 30 hundreds − 8 hundreds = 22 hundreds = 2200," or "3 thousands = 2 thousands + 10 hundreds; 2 thousands + 10 hundreds − 8 hundreds = 2 thousands + 2 hundreds = 2200."

**24 thousands − 8 hundreds = _____ .**

**Levels 0–4:** Not applicable.

**Level 5:** Student uses the traditional algorithm with understanding.

```
24000
 −800
23200
```

**Level 6:** Student says, "24 thousands − 8 hundreds = 23 thousands + 10 hundreds − 8 hundreds = 23 thousands + 2 hundreds = 23,200."

**1 million = _____ thousands.**

**Levels 0–4:** Not applicable.

**Level 5:** Student uses the traditional algorithm with understanding: $1000000 \div 1000 = 1000$.

**Level 6:** Student says, "1 million is 1000 thousands; that's how you go from the thousands period to the millions period."

# References

Baroody, A. J., & Ginsburg, H. P. (1990). "Children's Learning: A Cognitive View." In R. B. Davis, C. A. Maher, & N. Noddings (Eds.), *Constructivist Views on the Teaching and Learning of Mathematics. Journal for Research in Mathematics Education Monograph Number 4*: 51–64. Reston, VA: National Council of Teachers of Mathematics.

Battista, M. T. (1999). "The Mathematical Miseducation of America's Youth: Ignoring Research and Scientific Study in Education." *Phi Delta Kappan 80*(6): 424–433.

Battista, M. T. (2001). "How Do Children Learn Mathematics? Research and Reform in Mathematics Education." In Thomas Loveless (Ed.), *The Great Curriculum Debate: How Should We Teach Reading and Math?* Washington, DC: Brookings Press, pp. 42–84. (Based on a paper presented at the conference, "Curriculum Wars: Alternative Approaches to Reading and Mathematics." Harvard University, October 21–22, 1999.)

Battista, M. T. (2004). "Applying Cognition-Based Assessment to Elementary School Students' Development of Understanding of Area and Volume Measurement." *Mathematical Thinking and Learning 6*(2): 185–204.

Battista, M. T., & Clements, D. H. (1996). "Students' Understanding of Three-Dimensional Rectangular Arrays of Cubes." *Journal for Research in Mathematics Education 27*(3): 258–292.

Battista, M. T., Clements, D. H., Arnoff, J., Battista, K., & Borrow, C. V. A. (1998). "Students' Spatial Structuring and Enumeration of 2D Arrays of Squares." *Journal for Research in Mathematics Education 29*(5): 503–532.

Black, P., & Wiliam, D. (1998). "Raising Standards Through Classroom Assessment." *Phi Delta Kappan 80*(2): 139–148.

Bransford, J. D., Brown, A. L., & Cocking, R. R. (1999). *How People Learn: Brain, Mind, Experience, and School.* Washington, DC: National Research Council.

Buschman, Larry. (2001). "Using Student Interviews to Guide Classroom Instruction: An Action Research Project." *Teaching Children Mathematics* (December): 222–227.

Carpenter, T. P., & Fennema, E. (1991). "Research and Cognitively Guided Instruction." In E. Fennema, T. P. Carpenter, & S. J. Lamon (Eds.), *Integrating Research on Teaching and Learning Mathematics.* Albany: State University of New York Press, pp. 1–16.

Carpenter, T. P., Franke, M. L., Jacobs, V. R., Fennema, E., & Empson, S. B. (1998). "A Longitudinal Study of Invention and Understanding in Children's Multidigit Addition and Subtraction." *Journal for Research in Mathematics Education 29*(1): 3–20.

Carpenter, T. P., & Moser, J. M. (1984). "The Acquisition of Addition and Subtraction Concepts in Grades One Through Three." *Journal for Research in Mathematics Education 15*: 179–202.

Cobb, P., & Wheatley, G. (1988). "Children's Initial Understanding of Ten." *Focus on Learning Problems in Mathematics 10*(3): 1–28.

Cobb, P., Wood, T., Yackel, E., Nicholls, J., Wheatley, G., Trigatti, B., & Perlwitz, M. (1991). "Assessment of a Problem-Centered Second-Grade Mathematics Project." *Journal for Research in Mathematics Education 22*(1): 3–29.

De Corte, E., Greer, B., & Verschaffel, L. (1996). "Mathematics Teaching and Learning." In D. C. Berliner & R. C. Calfee (Eds.), *Handbook of Educational Psychology*. New York: Simon & Schuster Macmillan, pp. 491–549.

Fennema, E., & Franke, M. L. (1992). "Teachers' Knowledge and Its Impact." In D. A. Grouws (Ed.), *Handbook of Research on Mathematics Teaching*. Reston, VA: National Council of Teachers of Mathematics/Macmillan, pp. 127–164.

Fennema, E., Carpenter, T. P., Franke, M. L., Levi, L., Jacobs, V. R., & Empson, S. B. (1996). "A Longitudinal Study of Learning to Use Children's Thinking in Mathematics Instruction." *Journal for Research in Mathematics Education 27*(4): 403–434.

Fuson, K. C., Wearne, D., Hiebert, J. C., Murray, H. G., Human, P. G., Olivier, A. L., et al. (1997). "Children's Conceptual Structures for Multidigit Numbers and Methods of Multidigit Addition and Subtraction." *Journal for Research in Mathematics Education 28*(2): 130–162.

Greeno, J. G., Collins, A. M., & Resnick, L. (1996). "Cognition and Learning." In D. C. Berliner & R. C. Calfee (Eds.), *Handbook of Educational Psychology*. New York: Simon & Schuster Macmillan, pp. 15–46.

Hiebert, J., & Carpenter, T. P. (1992). "Learning and Teaching with Understanding." In D. A. Grouws (Ed.), *Handbook of Research on Mathematics Teaching*. Reston, VA: National Council of Teachers of Mathematics/Macmillan, pp. 65–97.

Lester, F. K. (1994). "Musing About Mathematical Problem-Solving Research: 1970–1994." *Journal for Research in Mathematics Education 25*(6): 660–675.

National Research Council. (1989). *Everybody Counts*. Washington, DC: National Academy Press.

Prawat, R. S. (1999). "Dewey, Peirce, and the Learning Paradox." *American Educational Research Journal 36*(1): 47–76.

Romberg, T. A. (1992). "Further Thoughts on the Standards: A Reaction to Apple." *Journal for Research in Mathematics Education 23*(5): 432–437.

Schoenfeld, A. C. (1994). "What Do We Know About Mathematics Curricula." *Journal of Mathematical Behavior 13*: 55–80.

Steffe, L. P., & D'Ambrosio, B. S. (1995). "Toward a Working Model of Constructivist Teaching: A Reaction to Simon." *Journal for Research in Mathematics Education 26*(2): 146–159.

Steffe, L. P. (1988). "Children's Construction of Number Sequences and Multiplying Schemes." In J. Hiebert & M. Behr (Eds.), *Number Concepts and Operations in the Middle Grades*. Reston, VA: National Council of Teachers of Mathematics, pp. 119–140.

Steffe, L. P. (1992). "Schemes of Action and Operation Involving Composite Units." *Learning and Individual Differences 4*(3): 259–309.

Steffe, L. P., & Kieren, T. (1994). "Radical Constructivism and Mathematics Education." *Journal for Research in Mathematics Education 25*(6): 711–733.

van Hiele, P. M. (1986). *Structure and Insight.* Orlando: Academic Press.

von Glasersfeld, Ernst. (1995). *Radical Constructivism: A Way of Knowing and Learning.* Washington, DC: Falmer Press.